The big book of low-cost training games

of

Other Books by Mary Scannell

The Big Book of Team-Motivating Games
The Big Book of Conflict Resolution Games
The Big Book of Virtual Team-Building Games
The Big Book of Brainstorming Games

Other Books by Jim Cain

Teamwork & Teamplay
The Revised and Expanded Book of Raccoon Circles
Teambuilding Puzzles
A Teachable Moment
The Ropework & Ropeplay Manual
Essential Staff Training Activities
Find Something to Do
It's All in the Cards

The big book

of

low-cost training games

Quick, Effective Activities That Explore Communication,
Goals Setting, Character Development, Team Building,
and More—and Won't Break the Bank!

Mary Scannell & Jim Cain

New York   Chicago   San Francisco   Lisbon   London   Madrid   Mexico City
Milan   New Delhi   San Juan   Seoul   Singapore   Sydney   Toronto

The McGraw·Hill Companies

1 2 3 4 5 6 7 8 9 10   QFR/QFR   1 9 8 7 6 5 4 3 2

ISBN   978-0-07-177437-6
MHID   0-07-177437-8

e-ISBN 978-0-07-178107-7
e-MHID   0-07-178107-2

Illustrations by Drake Carr and Jaclyn LaBarbera.
Photographs by Jim Cain.

This book is printed on acid-free paper.

Contents

4 Team- and Community-Building Activities 61

5 Puzzles and Games with Teachable Moments 133

6 Reviewing and Debriefing Techniques 199

7 The Right Stuff: Finding the References, Props, Tools, and Equipment You Need   229

Credits   239

Acknowledgments

Our sincere thanks go out to all the teams who have provided countless teachable moments and meaningful reflection in our training programs. We appreciate your participation and your contributions. We are grateful to the many companies who have entrusted us with their staff and trusted our training methods to help build knowledge and skills.

Thank you to Donya Dickerson, our editor at McGraw-Hill. Your insight and guidance provided the perfect amount of support throughout this endeavor. To Rena Copperman and her team, thank you for your expertise and hard work during the editing process. To Carolyn Wendt, we appreciate your eye for detail, which was vital for this project. To Julia Baxter and Sara Hendricksen, thank you for your enthusiasm around promoting our book!

Our special thanks go out to Drake Carr and Jaclyn LaBarbera for providing lively illustrations that add clarity and energy to our game descriptions.

And last, we are extremely grateful to Edward E. Scannell and Dr. John Newstrom for laying the foundation for this series of books that provide games to inspire, engage, and teach.

Preface

Return on investment (ROI) has become one of the key metrics in the corporate world. The ability to calculate this value not only for capital purchases of equipment but in regard to the training of employees is significant, especially in a business climate where all investments, including training, come under intense scrutiny.

It is not surprising then that in the field of employee training, some practices emerge that inherently offer better returns than others. It is exactly these techniques, these best practices, these unique activities, training simulations, and educational games that are the subject matter for this book: low-cost activities that offer high value, or using our initial metric, activities that produce a significant return on investment.

In the pages that follow, you'll find a substantial collection of simple, unique, and valuable training activities that you can use to instruct a variety of topics, from leadership to communication, and from creative problem solving to exploring character, plus many more. One common theme among this collection is that you won't need a substantial training budget to create or obtain the necessary equipment to lead these activities. In many cases, you'll find the materials you need at your local stationery store, hardware store, or shopping mall.

As you read through these activities, one thing to keep in mind is that a single activity can be used to teach more than a single subject or principle. A creative problem-solving challenge can be presented as a goal-setting activity. A communication activity can become a trust-building opportunity. Explore, create, try new things, and experiment with this collection of outstanding and engaging activities.

Now you have our collection of not only the best low-cost/high-value training activities we know, but some of the finest training activities in general, along with our best wishes for your next wildly successful training program.

"We have perfected the activities shared in this book by using them hundreds of times in decades of our programs, workshops and training events. We worked very hard on this project.

"We hope you'll read it with much pleasure."

—Mary Scannell
and Jim Cain

The big book

of

low-cost training games

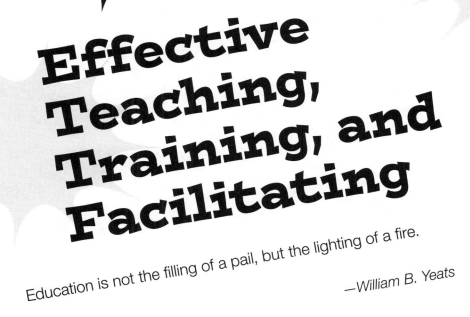

Effective Teaching, Training, and Facilitating

Education is not the filling of a pail, but the lighting of a fire.

—William B. Yeats

Whether you fit into the category of teacher, trainer, or facilitator (or any other title, such as group leader, manager, educator, presenter, or dozens of other choices), the suggestions in this first chapter will help you improve the presentation of your subject matter, increase the participation of your group, provide a format that is active and engaging, and become the best presenter you can be. Best of all, the activities featured in this book will help you present a wide variety of topics to your audience, using engaging methods that will help you meet your training needs, all at minimal cost.

While the classic definitions of teacher, trainer, and facilitator are unique in each case, there are some similarities in each profession. This chapter will share some of the best practices in each of these fields and in the process provide valuable tools you can use in your next program. In addition to the educational tools you'll find in this chapter, you'll also find several suggestions that are outside the educational realm but nonetheless have tremendous value when working successfully with groups. Not surprisingly, many of these ideas are perfectly applicable to the world of teaching, training, and facilitating groups.

On my first day of work as a design engineer for the Office Imaging Division of Eastman Kodak, I met Mike DeCecca. Mike walked into my office and remarked, "You're the new guy, huh?" I responded affirmatively. Without missing a beat, Mike immediately asked, "Do you know the Big Three?" I was a bit caught off guard by this impromptu quiz but quickly blurted out, "Ford, Chrysler, and General Motors?" After I answered Mike's question, he quickly pulled out his employee identification card and printed in neat handwriting on the back the Big Three:

1. What is it?
2. How is it done?
3. How can I use this to my advantage?

Mike confided in me that once I knew the Big Three, life would never be the same. Beyond the knowledge that you already have is a whole world of possibilities. Every time you see something, read something, or experience something, it becomes part of you, and you can use that knowledge and experience to your advantage in the future when presented with challenges and problems. Because I now know the Big Three, I am forever looking for new and better ways, sometimes from disciplines well outside my field of endeavor, and I'm using those new and better ways to my advantage whenever possible.

—Jim Cain

That is exactly what this chapter is all about. The Big Three. Things to read, consider, experience, and eventually make a part of your teaching, training, and facilitating. They are some of the most powerful ideas we know when it comes to improving the quality of your abilities to work with groups. We hope you enjoy this collection. Good luck!

Here is a list of the 20 ideas, suggestions, and pieces of advice that will be presented in this first chapter. May this information inspire you to be the best trainer, teacher, and facilitator you can be.

1. *Ancora Imparo*
2. The Power of Friendship and Positive Relationships
3. The SUCCES[s] Model
4. Three Important Things
5. The Four Fatal Assumptions of Leadership
6. Searching for the Right Book
7. Borrowing from the Field of Cooperative Learning
8. Educational Hooks and Triggers
9. The Experiential Learning Process
10. Peak Learning Strategies
11. The Six Rs
12. The Competency Ladder
13. The Seven-Minute Rule
14. Why Active Learning?
15. The Difference Between Short-Term and Long-Term Memory
16. The Three Primary Forms of Learning (Auditory, Visual, Kinesthetic)
17. Multiple Intelligences
18. Additional Hints, Suggestions, Ideas, Methods, Models, References, and Tools
19. H.A.L.T.
20. Squeeze the Lemon

1. *Ancora Imparo*

Ancora imparo: Yet I am learning.
　—*Michelangelo Buonarroti*

　This is a suitable wake-up call for the start of this book; the contents are designed to help you learn more, understand more, and do more.

　If you begin with the premise that there is still more you can learn, you form the foundation for a life of discovery To be a lifelong learner is to continue the process of learning, which continues to build new pathways in the brain, challenging old assumptions, considering new possibilities, and growing, always growing. The element of growth is so essential that it forms the first of the three critical elements of a high-performing organization.

　The illiterate of the 21st century will not be those who cannot read or write, but those who cannot learn, unlearn, and relearn.
　　　　　　　　　　　　　　　　　　　　　　—*Alvin Toffler*

　It is not the strongest of the species that survive, nor the most intelligent, but the one most responsive to change.
　　　　　　　　　　　　　　　　　　　　　　—*Charles Darwin*

2. The Power of Friendship and Positive Relationships

In this section on best practices, we explore the powerful combination of a worthy task, the opportunity for continual growth, and the power of positive relationships. The graphic illustrating these three components follows. Organizations that occupy the central region of this triple Venn diagram illustration maintain an excellent balance of all three components and achieve the highest quality of work environment as a result. And this visual model is also a road map for helping your organization move from where it is to where it would like to be. If you have too much task-oriented focus, try adding more growth and relationship opportunities. If you have plenty of work and a healthy balance of relationships, try adding some training or growth opportunities for your employees.

Not surprisingly, relationship building is the element most often viewed as critical but that is typically lacking in many organizations. Some of the most significant challenges in organizations around the world can be traced to relationship issues of trust, communication, familiarity, and teamwork. It is no mistake then that the following three scenarios are presented here. Armed with this information, you should be able to make a credible case for relationship building in your own organization, with even your most skeptical decision makers.

A colleague, friend, and fellow facilitator, Harvey Downey of Great Britain, once shared an experience that illustrates what some consider the most critical element of a high-performing organization: the ability to create and maintain positive relationships in the workplace.

When petty officers at the Royal Navy's basic training center HMS *Raleigh* near Cornwall were asked what significant factors made the difference between recruits passing or failing basic training, one drill instructor remarked, "If a recruit can make friends here, or even a borderline case can make even a single friend, they will probably make it through. If, however, they do not make friends, no matter how promising they are, they don't make it." Other instructors agreed.

The number one factor for successfully passing basic training was to *make a friend* during the process. Those who were successful built positive relationships during their basic training period. Many of those who were unsuccessful did not build friendships during this tremendously stressful period.

Ask yourself, "Where in my organization or even in my training program is there an opportunity for participants to make a friend?" If the answer is "Nowhere," you might want to reconsider the importance of this vital component and look for opportunities where you can help this happen.

To further expound on this idea (and to provide you with valuable ammunition that you might need to convince the decision makers in your organization's hierarchy), Tom Rath's book *Vital Friends* provides some very helpful numbers quantifying the effect that positive relationships have within an organization. Many of the training activities presented in this book will assist you in the process of forming relationships and building a positive culture in your workplace.

Of the significant statistics presented by Rath, three are unforgettable. First, that teenagers (including those in your workforce) spend nearly one-third of their time with friends, while the average for the rest of us is typically less than 10 percent. This number quantifies just how important relationships are to the youngest members of a workforce. Second, 96 percent of employees with at least three close friends at work reported that they were *extremely satisfied* with their lives and that the quality of their work life was *outstanding*! Again, the importance of relationships is statistically significant here. Finally and perhaps most importantly, from the Gallup poll that Rath cites throughout his book, the percentage of engaged employees in the general workforce is about 29 percent (with 54 percent disengaged and 17 percent actively disengaged). For employees without a friend at work, these numbers drop to 8 percent engaged, 63 percent disengaged, and 29 percent actively disengaged. But the good news is that for employees with a best friend at work, 56 percent are engaged! That is nearly double the average and a whopping eight times the engagement of those without friends in the workplace. More engaged workers and fewer disengaged workers sound like a win-win scenario to us.

By this point, we hope you are considering the idea that your organization can benefit by helping your employees create positive relationships within the workplace with their coworkers, supervisors, customers, vendors, and team members. Some may choose to call this teamwork, but it is as much *team bonding* as it is *team building*.

Let's consider one additional piece of ammunition before we leave this idea of the value of friendships and creating positive relationships in the workplace, one that directly relates to the financial savings of creating positive relationships.

The Theory of Group Development, as proposed by Bruce Tuckman of Ohio State University, can be expressed by naming the five stages of development as the forming, storming, norming, performing, and transforming stages. Suffice to say that most organizations would like to have their employees firmly within the performing stage of development. For every day their organization spends in the storming stage, inefficiencies abound, project deadlines are missed, and financial resources are drained without moving the corporation forward. Let's find out how to calculate what the storming stage costs an organization.

For most organizations, it is possible to calculate the salaries of all employees so that the cost of the entire organization can be known for any given day. As an example, let's consider an organization of 50 employees, all new to the organization and all working on the same project. As this group progresses through the stages of group development (from forming to storming to norming to performing to transforming), they require different skills for each stage. The storming stage can be one of the least cost-effective (and most frustrating) stages of group development. By spending a bit more time in the forming stage (where positive relationships begin), it is possible to actually shorten the amount of time required for the group to pass through the storming stage and move on to the norming and performing stages where real productivity and effort reside.

For every day your employees flounder in the storming stage, there is a cost to your organization. If you can shorten the total amount of time they stay in the storming process, you can save your organization some significant costs. If the cost of the 50 employees in our example above was

$100,000 per day, then the savings of a single day of storming behavior for each employee during a calendar year would be worth the same. If you can avoid the cost of even one day of storming by providing the opportunity for building positive relationships in the forming stage (often at a cost much less than the salaries of your 50 employees), wouldn't it be worth it?

3. The SUCCES[s] Model

In the best-selling book *Made to Stick: Why Some Ideas Survive and Others Die*, the authors Chip Heath and Dan Heath suggest a powerful mnemonic for ensuring that the members of your audience retain the information you share with them. The SUCCES[s] model presented in their book suggests that if you make your information Simple, Unexpected, Concrete, Credible, Emotional, and involve Stories, you'll provide the kind of learning environment where your audience will not only retain the information you present, but be able to use it in the future!

4. Three Important Things

Tom Andrews of the training company Pro Image (www.dare-to-grow .com) has a very simple but profound teaching model that should be part of every organization's training creed. Tom shares the following information with every participant at the very start of his training workshops:

1. I respect you.
2. Because I respect you, I am going to share the very best knowledge, tools, information, activities, and techniques that I know.
3. Because I respect you and share the best information that I know, I am going to hold you accountable to use this information to improve the world.

Tell this to your next group before you begin training, and they'll be more likely to listen carefully to the content you present. In fact, Tom's model above is a sure way to avoid what Clarke and Crossland call the four fatal assumptions of a leader, presented below.

5. The Four Fatal Assumptions of Leadership

While many of the theories, models, and instructional techniques shared in this section are built upon a positive theme to learning, education, and staff development, the following model is not. It concerns four fatal assumptions that can severely limit the effectiveness of your efforts to train and educate your staff. According to Boyd Clarke and Ron Crossland in their book *The Leader's Voice: How Your Communication Can Inspire Action and Get Results!*, effective leaders (including teachers, trainers, facilitators, directors, and managers) communicate using three distinct techniques: facts, emotions, and symbols. While these techniques are practical, useful, and generally effective, devotion to only a single technique can minimize the overall effectiveness of the message being presented. To be fully effective, the authors encourage leaders to communicate using all of these techniques. Clarke and Crossland further suggest that leaders often make the following (sometimes fatal) assumptions about their audiences.

1. That they understand the information being presented.
2. That they agree with the information being presented.
3. That they care about the information being presented.
4. That they will act accordingly using this information.

You could even make a case for adding an additional assumption prior to these four, namely that your audience is actually listening to you! In order to achieve the greatest return on the investment of your training dollars, it is important that you too avoid making these fatal assumptions during your next training program. How can you ensure that your audience is listening and that the information is getting through to them? How can you provide an open-door policy so that any staff member can voice his or her concern or agreement with a particular rule or regulation of your organization? How can you get your staff to care enough to act on the information they have received? How can you provide feedback during your training programs to ensure that your audience does not fall victim to these assumptions?

While the information contained in *The Leader's Voice* is now more than a decade old, it is fascinating that their fourth fatal assumption (that their audiences will act accordingly with the information they are presented) now ties in to some recent theories of brain function: namely that in addition to learning a specific skill, knowing where and when to apply this skill is essential to the training process. In other words, knowing *how* is one level, but knowing *where* is a higher-level skill.

6. Searching for the Right Book

With the dawn of electronic documents, audiobook recordings, and more recently electronic readers and tablet computers, there is an expanding variety of material to read. But finding the best documents, books, and resources to review can be problematic. There are almost too many resources out there, and with your limited time, you need to find the best resources quickly. So here are two recommendations for simplifying the task of finding web-based resources.

First, rather than searching using a single word (such as *teamwork*), try adding the letters *PDF* to any future search. In this way, instead of single hits to websites with information, you find documents filled with the information you need, in a whole and complete format. We recently used this technique to find www.archive.org (a repository of historically significant information and documents). At this website you can find entire books and documents, many that are over 100 years old. But the best news is that you can find a host of valuable group activities here, some of which date back hundreds of years.

Second, if you happen to be a person who enjoys visual information as well as text-based information, try switching from the text mode of most Internet search engines to the images mode. Now when you input a phrase, such as "team-building activities," instead of a long text list of websites, you'll receive images of groups in action. Clicking on a photograph or image of interest will take you to the website home of this image, with additional information.

7. Borrowing from the Field of Cooperative Learning

In the educational field of cooperative learning, Spencer Kagan is a prominent contributor. His work also includes workshops and conferences that cover the spectrum of learning, from multiple intelligences to classroom organization to team building. Within the pages of his numerous texts, you'll find a variety of techniques (and structures) for working with groups. Although much of the information presented is formatted for teachers in classroom situations, it is applicable for trainers (with adult learners) and group facilitators as well.

Which brings about an interesting insight, and one of the reasons that within the pages of this book we refer to trainers, teachers, and facilitators interchangeably. A good trainer can borrow activities from an elementary school playground book and adapt them for use in teaching the board of a major corporation. A text of group activities written in the 1700s can be transformed for the 21st century (and beyond). Nearly anything presented in a line can be bent into a circle, and vice versa. A small-group activity can be adapted to work with a large group. More to the point, a good trainer can take the elements of a good activity presented in the context of one group, and adapt it to make it suitable for a different group.

So the next time you find yourself browsing the bookshelves of your favorite bookstore, try wandering into a different section. You'll find ice-breakers in the corporate training environment but also in psychology (group interaction), education (classroom activities), after-school programming (circle time), summer camp staff training, scouting, sports management, and perhaps even a few more. Learn to look outside the realm of your traditional field and you may find some gems in other disciplines.

8. Educational Hooks and Triggers

If you have ever tried to remember something—the title of a book, a TV character's name, the words to a song—you have probably relied upon an educational hook or trigger to help you remember it. That is, remembering one thing helps you remember something else. Educational hooks are just like the hooks that you use to hold the tools in your workshop, your coat on a coatrack, or even your toothbrush in the bathroom. When you see the appropriate hook, even if the tool or jacket or toothbrush is missing, you know what belongs there. There is a connection between the hook and the object that it holds. By remembering the hook, you can also remember what it typically contains.

The Five Finger Rule is a great example of an educational hook. The hook is in fact the fingers of your right hand. Each finger represents a simple concept, as shown here:

- **The thumb: Be positive!** There is enough negativity in the world. You only have to watch the TV or read a newspaper to find it. Let's focus on the good things happening around us. Be positive!
- **The first or pointer finger: Don't point the finger at someone else.** Be responsible for yourself. It is human nature to make mistakes now and then, but we are terrible at covering them up. When you make a mistake, own up to it, and do your best to make it right.
- **The middle finger: It's all about respect.** Everyone deserves respect. Everyone!
- **The fourth or ring finger: Commitment.** To the team, to the situation, to the game.
- **And the last or pinky finger: Don't forget the little things.** Sometimes the smallest details can trip us up. Watch out for the little things, and the rest will take care of itself.

After teaching this simple rule, you can quiz your staff by holding up various fingers and asking them to repeat what each finger represents. They'll most likely be able to tell you each and every concept because you've given them a very simple hook.

The concept of an educational trigger is very similar to a hook. One word, phrase, or object helps you remember another important thing. Some bank and computer accounts use this information to assist you in case you forget your password or personal identification number (PIN), by asking such questions as "What was your mother's maiden name?" Often, before the customer finishes giving the answer to the bank's alternative question, that individual has remembered the password or PIN. Here are a few educational triggers below. Please add the missing word:

Peanut butter and _____.
Salt and _____.
Coffee with cream and _____.

Here, words and items are used to trigger your memory for another item. This style of memory tends to be easier to recall, because each item is connected to another important item, doubling the chances of the brain finding the information it needs. How many of the topics in your staff training are linked together, so that when your staff remembers one concept, they automatically remember another important piece of information as well?

Michael Brandwein in many of his books and workshops will use pneumonic devices to help his participants remember key concepts. These too are examples of educational triggers. For example, WIBYT stands for "Write it before you talk." The act of writing down information is a more engaged level of learning than just listening. Sometimes, in the act of writing down the concept being taught, staff members will have sufficient time to consider the concept themselves and draw their own conclusion, rather than jumping to ask additional questions. WIBYT isn't just a pneumonic device; it is a great idea that will encourage your audience to think more deeply about the information you are presenting.

9. The Experiential Learning Process

David Kolb is most often credited with his work related to the experiential learning process, which states that individuals and groups progress through their experiences. One of the greatest educational takeaways from this model is the fact that simply experiencing an educational moment is an incomplete way of learning. Not until learners have reflected on and applied this learning can they be said to have truly learned the material presented.

In application to training, it is important not only to share the necessary information and knowledge with your attendees but also to allow them to reflect on this information, and best of all, be given an opportunity to actually use this new knowledge in a genuine situation. Role-plays, practice events, group work, and teach-backs are all helpful ways to prepare your staff to use the knowledge they have gained successfully.

An example of this theory from medical school is the "See one, do one, teach one" approach to learning medical procedures. First students observe. Next they perform the task themselves. Finally, students achieve the level of ability where they can effectively teach others this skill. The student has truly become the master. And best of all, students in this scenario are proficient enough to actually use the knowledge they have acquired, just as you would like your staff to do.

10. Peak Learning Strategies

The work of M. J. Ellis, Yerkes and Dodson, and others has explored the theme of optimal arousal or peak learning. Simply stated, students achieve the highest levels of interest in learning when the skills they presently possess and the skills they are required to master are at an optimal ratio. If their interest level is too low (they cannot see the application or need for the subject matter), their ability to retain and use the information is minimized. The more optimal the interest level, the more likely they will retain and apply the information they receive. There is an upper limit as well. Too high an arousal level, and students are unable to focus. The optimal arousal model is often referred to as the Yerkes–Dodson law or the inverted-U theory, and relates arousal level to performance. Sports psychologists have used the optimal arousal theory for achieving high performance in athletes. And by *optimal,* they do not mean *maximum* arousal. Rather, the goal is the optimum level of arousal (focus, intensity, readiness) for the situation.

Thinking of your past staff training experiences, when was your audience most interested, focused, and ready to learn? Keep a journal this coming year, and make notes after each specific section of your training programs. Mark which training topics could use a boost in participant focus, and which ones are just fine. Use some of the activities and methods in this book to improve the training topics that you decide need higher involvement.

Mihaly Csikszentmihalyi's research on flow (the sweet spot between boredom and anxiety) is another way of expressing this same phenomenon, and not surprisingly, it also has a sports psychology component. When you provide an atmosphere of learning that moves beyond boredom for students and does not exceed the level that would cause anxiety, you will have achieved the optimal learning environment. Most students don't consciously realize that they are in flow until after they have left it again. "Wow, I was really focused back there, wasn't I?"

For more reading on this subject, try an Internet search using terms such as "optimal arousal learning" or "Yerkes–Dodson law." You can also read *Finding Flow* by Mihaly Csikszentmihalyi, or *Beyond Boredom and Anxiety* by the same author.

11. The Six Rs

In her office for the C5 Youth Foundation (www.c5leaders.org), our colleague Clare-Marie Hannon has a small sign with the six Rs. Make sure when you tell your employees about specific rules and regulations in your organization, you also tell them why these are necessary, and do so in a respectful way. Simply stated, if you create rules and regulations without reasons and respect, you'll get resentment and rebellion from your staff.

The Six Rs

$$\frac{(\text{Rules} + \text{Regulations}) - (\text{Reasons} + \text{Respect})}{(\text{Resentment} + \text{Rebellion})}$$

12. The Competency Ladder

Before you begin teaching your staff any concept, consider the following ladder model. Each step of this model signifies an increase in the skill level of the participant. The higher the level, the greater the ability of the student to successfully use the knowledge gained. You should ask yourself before you begin writing your training plan, "What level do I want my staff to achieve as a result of this training?" If it is acceptable for your staff to have a basic awareness of a concept (for example, staff should park their cars in the parking area behind the maintenance building), then you probably can move quickly through this information and expect that most of your staff will park their vehicles appropriately. If, on the other hand, you need your staff to exhibit a high level of mastery on a particular subject (moving campers to a safe location in the event of high winds, which are likely to occur later this week), then as an instructor, teacher, and facilitator, you need to use educational techniques that will move your staff beyond simple awareness and knowledge, and well into competence and perhaps even mastery (perfection) of this particular piece of knowledge. Concepts that demand mastery from

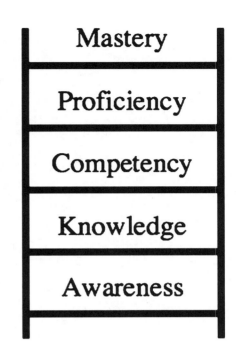

your staff require mastery in their presentation to your staff.

The concept "See one, do one, teach one" from earlier in this section is applicable here as well. "Each one teach one" is another way of expressing this same philosophy. Students move up the competency ladder when they are presented with a new concept (awareness) and given the opportunity to explore and practice this concept (knowledge and competency) and to perfect their ability to the point where they are able to share this knowledge with others (proficiency and mastery). So if you want mastery from your staff on a particular subject, be sure your teaching presentation mirrors this level of ability and allows the opportunity for students to perfect their abilities rather than merely observe the subject.

In a similar fashion to the competency ladder, there is another model that can help a trainer plan the appropriate amount of content to actually deliver the necessary outcomes to an organization. Several facilitators and trainers have mentioned that they were considered failures by organizations for not delivering cultural change (and group behavioral changes) even though these same organizations rejected their proposals for sufficient time, resources, and curriculum latitude to actually effect such

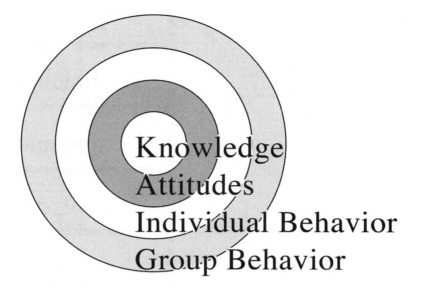

Knowledge
Attitudes
Individual Behavior
Group Behavior

changes. Many organizations want such culture-shifting behavior in their work teams, but few fully understand the level of training actually necessary to accomplish it.

Consider the target model shown here. The amount of time, curriculum, effort, and indeed difficulty encountered to effect changes in the concepts noted in each ring increases as you move further outward from the center. Like the competency ladder, basic knowledge is achievable with a limited investment. For higher levels of competency, additional effort is required. In the case of this target model, the greater the magnitude of change required, the greater the difficulty in accomplishing such a change. Don't make the mistake of trying to change the group behavior of an entire staff in 20 minutes of lecture.

13. The Seven-Minute Rule

In a standard training environment, most of the intellectual content is transmitted via visual and auditory stimulation. Not surprisingly, when such content is delivered in dim lighting, as in a computer-generated slide show, the relaxation response of the audience generally increases past the learning response level. To combat such an outcome, many teachers, trainers, and facilitators will incorporate some level of activity within the program. Some would argue that movement is essential to the learning process, and we agree. That is why we have contributed so many active activities in this book. But even movement has its limitations when it comes to the attention span of participants in a learning environment.

While a significant amount of the research related to attention span is directed toward children, even adults benefit from a change during the learning process. As a general rule of thumb, the attention span is related to the age of the individual. An 8-year-old has an attention span of about 8 minutes for a single task, and a 12-year-old, 12 minutes. There is a maximum of about 22 minutes, even for adults.

If you think back to the training activities that most captured your interest or maintained the highest levels of energy for a group of participants, a majority were probably conducted in less than ten minutes. This is not to say that some longer activities are not valuable; they just require a longer span of attention than is optimal for many people in a training environment. This can be especially true for one of the basic elements of a training program, the opening icebreaker.

When given the choice between participation in a group ice-breaking activity or answering the latest text or voice message on their cell phone, most people would choose the latter. Icebreakers can be painful, silly, unavoidable, and thus unproductive moments in the learning process. But they could be so much more. To help refine your list of icebreakers and to provide you with more than a dozen "painless" ones, you'll find a collection of our favorite and best opening activities in this book. But keep in mind the following simple recommendation: Keep any single icebreaker or opening activity to a maximum of seven minutes.

Organize the size of your groups so that any opening activity is less than seven minutes in length. For example, opening introductions with a group of 20 people could easily take 20 minutes or more. It is better to organize a group this size into three subgroups and limit the total introduction time to about seven minutes.

If you happen to have set aside 30 minutes for an icebreaker activity, you can incorporate four different fast-paced icebreakers in this same time, and keep the energy of your audience at a much higher level as a result. Seven minutes max. That's it!

14. Why Active Learning?

Simply stated, active learning is just that: learning in an active and engaging manner. The role of the teacher becomes that of a facilitator. Knowledge isn't something that is poured into learners, but rather something they explore and find for themselves. Through the process of inquiry, investigation, group work, discussions, and other active learning opportunities that move beyond lectures and slide presentations, learners are given a more active role in their own education. You expect your staff to think on their feet, so why not train them on the feet? Three experts in education and brain function have this to say about active learning:

> As the bottom gets numb-er, the brain gets dumber!
> —*Marcia L. Tate*

> Your brain can only absorb what your butt can endure!
> —*Gabe Campbell*

> Movement is the door to learning.
> —*Paul Dennison*

By including active learning in your training sessions, you'll engage your participants more deeply by providing a sensory-rich learning environment. Edgar Dale's work on memory and retention of information suggests that the greater the level of involvement or immersion of the student in the learning process, the greater the retention of the information given. While most forms of conventional learning are somewhat passive (lecture, computer-based learning, PowerPoint presentations, slide shows, reading), there are other choices.

Given the finite amount of time you have available to train your staff, and no doubt the extensive amount of material you have to cover during this process, chances are you would not only like to complete the delivery of the information you have at hand, but ensure that your audience actually retains this information and is able to apply it in the future. And sometimes these two facets (time and the total amount of information) are at odds with each other. You are going to need some help to make this happen, and here it is.

What you will find in this book is a collection of tools and techniques that you can use to create a sensory-rich and active learning environment during your staff training sessions. Remember, the greater the number of methods used to convey information to your staff, the greater their potential for being able to recall this information and actually apply that knowledge in the right situation, at the right time. Best of all, there are dozens of valuable techniques here, so you can vary the methods you use throughout your staff training program, to keep the information interesting, and the presentation of this information continuously changing and engaging.

15. The Difference Between Short-Term and Long-Term Memory

The difference between short-term and long-term memory in just 20 seconds! That's all, 20 seconds. If you can get your staff to manipulate a concept in their minds for 20 seconds, you can move that concept from their short-term memory to a long-term memory location. Less than 20 seconds—short-term memory. More than 20 seconds—20 years or more!

Consider for yourself how many times you have been given a telephone number, but before you could write it down, you've lost some of the digits. Chances are you forgot some of those digits before 20 seconds had passed.

One of the activities in this book, Active Quotations, makes use of a group deliberating the correct order of words in a quote they do not yet know. By manipulating the cards containing these words (which generally takes much more than just 20 seconds), members of the group not only retain the message of the quote, but also can repeat it word for word and will continue to be able to do so now that it resides in their long-term memory.

In regard to your training sessions, any concept that you present for less than 20 seconds is likely to be heard by your participants but unlikely to be retained by them unless you do something more to engage their memory system! Try the activity Active Quotations for your organization's mission statement, vision statement, or goals, and chances are your staff will remember them long after the activity is completed.

16. The Three Primary Forms of Learning (Auditory, Visual, Kinesthetic)

While additional educational techniques are more common these days, there remain some traditional learning methods that endure because of their value and effectiveness. *Auditory* techniques include teaching by voice, using stories, electronically stored voices, music, books on tape and CD, podcasts, MP3 files, and other person-to-person or electronic means. Sharing your favorite campfire story with your trainees is an example of auditory learning. *Visual* techniques include visual aids such as graphics, illustrations, models, graphs, pictures, and 3-D items that you can pass around the group. *Kinesthetic* learning includes movement of all kinds. Learning how to serve a volleyball and how to tie a knot using a short length of rope are examples of kinesthetic learning.

17. Multiple Intelligences

While the work of Howard Gardner is most often credited with defining the current eight accepted styles of multiple intelligences or learning styles, some find this information a bit pedagogical. Thomas Armstrong does an excellent job of interpreting multiple intelligence theory and making it accessible for those of us who would like to utilize these techniques without obtaining a doctoral degree in education first. Armstrong's book *Multiple Intelligences in the Classroom* is highly recommended.

In this and other sources on multiple intelligence learning methods, you'll find that there are (currently) eight varieties of intelligences that you can address in your teachings: logical-mathematical, bodily-kinesthetic, visual spatial, linguistic, musical, interpersonal (knowledge of others), intrapersonal (knowledge of self), and natural-environmental. In addition, there is some effort under way to include other potential intelligence forms, including existentialism, mechanical aptitude, and humor.

For many teachers, educators, and trainers, investigating these eight styles, although interesting, is difficult given a standardized curriculum, and impossible given the time provided to explore such techniques. Luckily active learning techniques can be used to explore ALL of these intelligences. And best of all, the activities mentioned in this book address all of the multiple intelligence styles.

18. Additional Hints, Suggestions, Ideas, Methods, Models, References, and Tools

Here are a few more ideas for continuing to improve the environment of your training sessions and to create a positive culture within your organization. Think of this as a list of opportunities, each one capable of improving the quality of your next training program.

For starters, make friends with your local library. No doubt you have a very busy season ahead, and staff training is just one part of it. Before the season arrives, visit your local library or bookstore, and invest some time reading the books mentioned in this section. Many of the books referenced here were borrowed from the local public library. You can also find quite a bit of information about these subjects on the Internet.

Research-Based Strategies to Ignite Student Learning: Insights from a Neurologist and Classroom Teacher by Judy Willis provides a unique collection of advice from someone who is both a teacher and a neurologist.

For each different way you learn something, another memory pathway is created in the brain. Each pathway then becomes one more possible way you have of remembering and using that information. Think of it like this. The first time you learn the directions to a location, say a nearby hardware store, you tend to begin with landmarks that you already know, eventually venturing off to new routes. After you have driven these routes a few times, you find other ways of getting there—back roads, alternate routes, and shortcuts. Now you have multiple ways of achieving the same goal, to get to the hardware store. So it is with learning something. The more pathways you have, the more opportunities you have for remembering, or in the case of our example, actually arriving at the hardware store.

Paul Dennison's work in "Brain Gym" techniques is presented in several of his books, including *Brain Gym: Revised Teacher's Edition* (co-authored with Gail Dennison). The idea that physical movement prepares the body and awakens the mind for learning is a concept that you can use during your staff trainings. Nearly every teacher, trainer, and facilitator has witnessed the drop in energy that most audiences experience after lunch. Brain Gym techniques can reenergize and refocus your group. Several of the activities in this book specifically use movement to build energy and engagement in the group. Try the Story Stretch or the Leadership Dance the next time staff members begin to lose their energy. You can also use many of the Brain Gym exercises to energize your staff.

One of the most recent books by Paul Dennison about Brain Gym is *Brain Gym and Me: Reclaiming the Pleasure of Learning*. Also, see Carla Hannaford's book *Smart Moves: Why Learning Is Not All in Your Head* for even more ideas about the value of movement in active learning. If you want to evaluate the effectiveness of your staff-training program, read Donald Kirkpatrick and James Kirkpatrick's book *Evaluating Training Programs: The Four Levels* (3rd edition). A chapter on experiential and outdoor training was written by Richard Wagner, an outstanding educator and experiential learning specialist, now at the University of Wisconsin at Whitewater. For one of the most interesting recent books on training, read *Telling Ain't Training* by Harold Stolovitch and Erica Keeps. Of all the books we researched during the writing of this book, this one stood out for the variety of interesting training information shared. Here is one example of how the work of Stolovitch and Keeps and Michael Brandwein connect.

The information contained in your short-term memory begins to fade in about 20 seconds and the number of informational chunks this memory can retrain is only five to nine independent pieces. Telephone numbers are seven digits long for a reason! If you can parcel information in your training sessions into connected chunks rather than single pieces of information, your staff will have a much easier time remembering. Consider as an example Brandwein's use of mnemonics in the WIBYT example from the Educational Hooks and Triggers section in this chapter. "Write it before you talk" is five pieces of information, but WIBYT is just one. No wonder mnemonics are such a useful memory device!

Joanna Carolan's book *Little World: A Book About Tolerance* makes an inspirational reading for your staff training program. It is a perfect lead-in for discussion on diversity and tolerance. Which do you think is more likely in the next ten years: that your community, workforce, and staff will be more ethnically diverse, or less? For anyone answering more, *Little World* is a good place to start.

The book *Everybody Needs a Rock* by Byrd Baylor tells a great story about choosing the perfect rock for yourself. Read this one to your staff while standing near a riverbed with thousands of rocks all around. While choosing the perfect rock may not be a specific goal of your next staff training session, this book does provide a great example of creating a sensory-rich learning environment. Ask several members of your staff to read a page or two of this book. Chances are everyone will be engaged during this part of the program. And the rock they choose will become a lifelong memento of this experience.

Edgar Dale's work using various presentation skills and measuring his students' retention of this information is an example of the power of multi-sensory learning tools. His "Cone of Learning" is often used to advocate using higher levels of activity to increase the retention of information in traditional learning environments. And while there is some controversy related to his model, it does have parallel significance with some more recent brain research that suggests creating multiple pathways in the brain (by teaching in a variety of ways) improves retention and recollection of information.

Passive learning generally has a lower level of retention than more active techniques. Current active training techniques include using song lyrics, videos (including DVDs and Internet sources of media like YouTube), graphics, music, movies, TV shows, stories, text messages, and even photographs from your cell phone. One resource, the Teach with Movies website (www.teachwithmovies.org), shows how recent and classic movie clips can be used to reinforce training topics. If you use computer-generated slide shows, there is a slide-show-sharing website (www.slideshare.net) where you can find hundreds of training themes and slide shows, including one of the more interesting global awareness slide shows, "Shift Happens."

Marcia L. Tate's work related to brain research and growing dendrites through active learning is presented in her book *"Sit and Get" Won't Grow Dendrites: 20 Professional Learning Strategies That Engage the Adult Brain.* Tate mentions strategies for improving the learning process, including facilitation instead of teaching, creative and artistic expression, field trips, games, graphics, humor, haptic (tactile) objects, metaphors, movement, music, drama, storytelling, technology, visual aids, and journaling.

19. H.A.L.T.

If you are Hungry, Angry, Lonely, or Tired, it is time for a break. Trying to push a group or an individual through any one of these situations has a diminishing return on your investment. It is far better to take a break, rectify the issue at hand, and then return to the discussion or topic at a later time.

During any training program, there generally comes a time when the energy of the group declines. Be aware of this probability and have a strategy ready. As an example, try using an energizer from this book (such as the Leadership Dance) to reinvigorate your audience before continuing your training agenda.

20. Squeeze the Lemon

Consider this analogy: Getting more out of the style of training activities presented in this book is a bit like making lemonade. You grab a few lemons, squeeze them, get some juice, and make lemonade. Life is good. But if you squeeze harder, you get more.

So it is with not only the activities in this book, but many of the training activities you already know. If you just squeeze harder, you'll get more out of them as well.

So throughout this book, you'll find additional insights and hints to help you get more out of each activity. As much as we can, we'll show you how to squeeze more out of these activities. As authors, our goal is not only for you to be able to read and understand the information we present in this book but also be able to use that knowledge to present these activities in your next training program, in a manner that is valuable and ultimately successful.

2

Getting the Most from the Activities in This Book

It is a happy talent to know how to play.

—Ralph Waldo Emerson

With the activities in this book, you can actively explore a wide variety of valuable topics in your next program. But there are additional opportunities if you choose to use these activities *and* create an environment conducive for conversation and reflection after each activity. As an example, consider the following real-life case.

During a team-building session, author Jim Cain was asked by a supervisor to incorporate an activity that addressed some of the issues related to absenteeism in the workplace. She went on to explain that when an employee was unexpectedly absent, they often hired a temp worker for the day, but this worker seldom was as efficient as the absent employee, and only a fraction of the work was accomplished as planned, leaving other members of the team stressed and frustrated. He didn't have a ready activity for this particular topic but instead removed a critical piece of equipment from an upcoming activity. When team members asked where the missing piece was, he replied, "Oh, they called in sick today. I guess we'll have to do the best we can without them." This situation prompted a discussion from the group related to absenteeism that went on to address many of the key concerns of the supervisor. When the activity and discussion were finished, the supervisor looked at him and remarked, "That was a perfect way to create a teachable moment. Thank you."

In this case, it wasn't the actual focus of the activity to teach skills related to absenteeism, but rather the activity created an experience that the participants could reflect upon. In this case, it was the reflection after the experience that provided the valuable lesson.

John Dewey, the great educational theorist, wrote the book *Experience and Education,* and implied that experience is a critical part of the learning process. But others would challenge Dewey in that experience alone is not all that is required for learning. Clifford Knapp, David Kolb, Bert Horwood, John Luckner, Reldan Nadler, and many others have gone to great lengths to validate that the experiential learning cycle requires the inclusion of a review or reflection component as well.

Bert Horwood, in a passionate keynote speech at the Association for Experiential Education Northwest regional conference, once asked, "Do we learn from experience?" Most members of the audience nodded their heads, affirming this thought. "No!" cried Horwood as he slammed his fist onto the podium. "We learn when we REFLECT on that experience!"

While it is difficult to portray that level of passion in print, as authors we are no less passionate about the opportunities available here, using both the activities themselves and the post-activity reviewing and reflection opportunities that further complete the learning process.

Our job then, as trainers, teachers, and facilitators, is to create teachable moments for our participants, employees, and students. Sure, we can use an activity to explore communication issues, but when we actively reflect on that experience and then apply the knowledge gained, we extend the value of the activity greatly. In short, the action/reflection/application cycle (most commonly referred to as the experiential learning cycle) is completed.

You may find, as we have over the years, that every time you facilitate an activity, you gain insight as to how to lead a more meaningful debriefing discussion for that activity. You may also find that your participants contribute to a deeper level of reflection. While we have provided questions to help you lead your post-activity discussion, be sure to note the process your participants create while they navigate through the activity. You will discover that your discussions are as diverse as your participants.

We also provide rules and guidelines for the activities, which can be tightened or relaxed at your discretion. The rules provide an opportunity for greater levels of challenge. When you throw the rules out altogether, or when competition takes over and teams become overly concerned with winning to the point of cheating, rich and meaningful activities run the risk of becoming silly games.

On the following pages, you'll find a description of each of the activities presented in this book, together with specific teachable moments you can create. You'll also find additional information related to group size, time span, props required, and other logistical concerns to help you maximize the value of each of the activities you choose to use. You can accommodate a group size larger than the ideal group size shown in the charts below, simply by creating multiple groups, each with their own collection of props or equipment.

Opening Activities, Energizers, and Painless Icebreakers

Activity Name	Description, Theme, Teachable Moment	Group Size	Time (Minutes)	Props
The Story of Your Name	Creating an Atmosphere of Respect	< 30	20–40	None
Over Here!	Creating an Atmosphere of Inclusion	> 20	10–20	None
Walk and Talk	Painless Icebreaker with a Partner	2	5–8	None
The Big Question	Painless Icebreaker, Conversation Starter	> 10	10	Handout
The Big Answer	Finding Solutions to Life's Problems	> 10	10	Handout
Story Stretch	Warm-Up Activity, Leadership	Groups of 8	10–15	None
Raccoon Circles— Wrapped Around My Finger	Painless Icebreaker	< 8	10–20	Raccoon Circle
Raccoon Circles— Where Ya From, Where Ya Been?	Geographic Icebreaker	< 8	10–20	Raccoon Circle
Raccoon Circles— Twice Around the Block	Painless Icebreaker	< 8	10–20	Raccoon Circle
Raccoon Circles— My Lifeline	Highlights, Icebreaker	< 8	10–20	Raccoon Circle
Raccoon Circles— My Life's a Circle	Highlights, Icebreaker	< 8	10–20	Raccoon Circle
Raccoon Circles—The Goal Line	Goal Setting	< 30	10–20	Raccoon Circles

Team- and Community-Building Activities

Activity Name	Description, Theme, Teachable Moment	Group Size	Time	Props
Bobsled Team	Teamwork, Communication	Groups of 4	10	None
Community Juggling	Coordination, Communication, Teamwork	< 20	20	Props
Character Cards	Character Discussion	Multiple groups of 8 to 10	20	Index Cards, Masking Tape, or Rope
Peteca	Energy, Change, Teamwork	10 Groups of 8 to 10	20	Petecas
Back Writing	Communication, Feedback	Multiple groups of 5	20	Index Cards, Markers
"Un-Blind" Square	Communication, Leadership, Problem Solving	< 20	20	Long Rope
Shoelaces	Teamwork, Creative Problem Solving, Communication	2	10–20 minutes	Shoes with Laces
Bull Ring Candelabra	Problem Solving, Teamwork	18 to 36	30	Bull Rings
Alphabet Soup	Quality Improvement, Goal Setting	5–20	20	Index Cards, Ropes
Snowflakes	Communication, Listening	Any	5	Paper
Lighthouse	Communication, Trust, Teamwork	Any	10	Props
Sunny Side Up	Problem Solving, Timing, Teamwork	Multiple groups of 6–8	15	Tarps, Tennis Balls
Inside Out	Problem Solving, Teamwork, Integrity	6–8	10	Raccoon Circle
The Leadership Dance	A Kinesthetic Leadership Opportunity	Any	15	Music
The Trust Drive	Trust, Feedback, Relationship Building	Any	15–20	Trust Drive Script
Magic Carpet	Goal Setting, Creative Problem Solving	Multiple groups of 8 to 10	15	Magic Carpets
Engineering 101	Communication, Creativity	Multiple groups of 8 to 10	20	Construction Materials
Changing Places	Collaboration, Problem Solving	6–8	30	Paper
Zoom	Communication, Problem Solving	< 30	20–30	Zoom Book
A Knot Between Us	Problem Solving, Teamwork	6–20	10–30	Ropes, Racoon Circle

Puzzles and Games with Teachable Moments

Activity Name	Description, Theme, Teachable Moment	Group Size	Time	Props
Active Quotations	Linguistic Challenge, Long-Term Memory	< 20	10–15	Index Cards
The Missing Link	Building Consensus, Listening	< 30	10	2 Ropes
Word Circles	Linguistic Challenge, Teamwork	< 25	10–15	Index Cards
13 Clues	Solving a Mystery with Clues	< 10	20	Index Cards
Blind Shapes	Communication, Trust, Problem Solving	< 15	30–45	Shapes
Handcuffs	Problem Solving, Teamwork, Relationships	2	10	Short Ropes
16-Card Puzzle	Creative Problem Solving	< 7	10	Playing Cards
Modern Hieroglyphics	Linguistic Challenges, Communication	Any	15	Handout
Arrowheads	Working with Minimal Resources	< 5	10	Arrowheads
A Quick Study	Creative Problem Solving, Simplicity	> 20	10	White Board
Nail Puzzle	Problem Solving, Relationships	< 7	10	Nail Puzzles
Tangrams	Creative Problem Solving, Diversity	< 10	10–20	Tangrams
PVC Construction	Teamwork, Problem Solving	< 7	10–20	PVC Tubes
"I'm In" Games	Creative Problem Solving	> 10	10–20	None

Closing, Reviewing, and Debriefing Techniques

Activity Name	Description, Theme, Teachable Moment	Group Size	Time	Props
Pairing and Sharing	Debriefing Technique with Partners	Any	5	None
The Magic Pot	Imaginary Debriefing Technique	< 30	10	None
The Fishbowl	Reviewing Technique	< 20	10	Long Rope
Four-Minute Team	Teambuilding, Team Bonding	< 20	4	Stopwatch
Step into the Circle	Finding Your Voice, Having Your Say	< 20	10	Long Rope
Body Part Debrief	Metaphorical Debriefing Technique	< 20	10	Props
Playing Card Debrief	Metaphorical Reviewing Technique	< 20	10	Playing Cards
Partner Watch	Feedback and Reviewing Technique	2	5	None
Highs and Lows	Reviewing Framework with Categories	< 20	10	Framework
Tweeting	A Concise Summary of the Experience	Any	10	Handout

3

Opening Activities, Energizers, and Painless Icebreakers

The beginning is the most important part of the work.

—Plato

The Story of
Your Name

OBJECTIVE

• To create an atmosphere of respect

Group Size

Less than 30

Materials

None

Time

20 to 40 minutes

Procedure

In a world economy with greater and greater cultural diversity in our organizations and communities, it is increasingly important to build an atmosphere of respect if we are to support the outstanding relationships that are required for a high-performance work environment. One of the first ways to build positive relationships, or conversely to destroy them, is in the manner in which we identify each other. To give significance to someone's name is to give significance to that person as well.

As a name game, the Story of Your Name is a simple method for helping people recall interesting stories about the other members of their group and from these stories remember their names as well. But in addition to the simple task of remembering the names of group members, the Story of Your Name creates an atmosphere of respect in a world of continuously increasing diversity.

What do you think is more likely to happen in the next ten years? That the community you live in (work in) will become more or less culturally diverse? For many of us, the diversity of our communities, both corporate and geographic, is increasing. That means that the opportunity for us to interact with others of significantly different backgrounds, customs, languages, and cultures is also increasing. Learning how to respectfully call another person by name is a very convenient initial skill in building community and positive relationships.

Everyone has a story related to their name. Some of us are named after another member of our family, a close friend of our parents, or perhaps someone famous. Many men and women know what their name would have been, had they been born the opposite gender. Our middle names are significant too. For this activity, invite everyone to share the story of their name: how they came to have it; if they like it or not; who else has their name; and what nicknames they might have. At the end of their story, encourage participants to end with the phrase "I'd like you to call me [*their name of choice here*]." In this way, everyone will have the opportunity to say how they would ideally like to be addressed, and what is positive about their name. This is a very powerful activity indeed, and one that is sure to build an atmosphere of respect in the workplace.

To begin, the facilitator should be the first to tell the story of his or her name, providing an example of the content (and duration) practical for this activity. While this activity requires no equipment, it does require significant time. When practical, especially for groups of 40 or fewer people, perform this activity in one large group, so that everyone has the opportunity to learn the names of all other members of the group. As an estimate of the total time required for this activity, most participants speak for one to two minutes. For groups greater than 40 people, this would require over an hour's worth of time. For groups larger than 40, you may want to consider splitting into multiple smaller groups to fit within your allotted time.

As an example, several graduate students from universities around the world attended a technical conference at Penn State. One student from China had arrived in the United States only two days earlier, and her language skills were challenging. But we did manage to introduce her to ice cream from the on-campus ice-cream store, which quickly became her favorite American food.

At dinner, she introduced herself to our group and her name was very unusual. When asked her what her name meant, she mentioned that everyone in her family had great names. "My name means 'all the colors of the rainbow' in my native language," she said. "What does your name mean?"

What followed was a lengthy introduction by all the members of our group, telling us all the interesting facts, stories, and unusual consequences of their names. And best of all, these stories made it very easy to remember everyone's name throughout the conference.

Over Here!

Group Size

More than 20

Materials

None

Time

10 to 20 minutes

Procedure

If you only choose two activities from this book, the Story of Your Name (which creates an atmosphere of respect) and this activity, Over Here! (which creates an atmosphere of inclusion), would be our recommendations. These two simple activities can dramatically improve the culture in any organization.

Over Here! begins with groups of approximately five people standing in a small circle and separate from other nearby groups. If helpful, each group can be standing within a Raccoon Circle or rope circle. The facilitator introduces the activity by informing each group that they have the opportunity to find out a bit more about each other. Tell the groups:

"I'm going to ask you to point to the person in your group who is the tallest. When I say, 'One, two, three,' I want you to wave good-bye to this person and say, 'See ya!' Once this person leaves your circle, that person becomes a free agent. But your group has lost a person. The way to invite someone else to join your group is to yell, 'Over here, over here, over here!'"

At this point, one person from each group departs and joins another group.

"Okay, here are a few ground rules. First, is it okay to get the same person back? Yes! Is it okay to get more than one person? Sure! Can you go out and recruit if you have to? Yes. Do you know the difference between recruitment and abduction? Recruitment is a noncontact activity. You can invite people to join your group, but you cannot grab them and drag them into your circle."

Once your audience understands these rules, you can continue the activity with some of the categories shown here. The *free agent* can be invited to any group. Some groups will soon overflow their circle boundary. Other groups may soon lose all of their members. Some groups may choose to combine forces. Some groups on the outside perimeter may choose to move their circle to a better location. Lots of strategies are possible here.

- Who has traveled the farthest distance to be here?
- Who has the most brothers and sisters?
- Who has the longest or shortest hair?
- Who has visited the most countries?
- Who is wearing the coolest watch?
- Who is wearing the most jewelry?
- Who speaks the most languages?
- Who owns the most pets?

Don't underestimate the power of this simple activity. By creating a situation where your audience members feel comfortable joining *any* group, you can avoid some of the traditional separation that can occur between various segments of a team. In some organizations, for example, it is not uncommon for different work groups to form their own silo or clique. If you include Over Here! with these groups, you'll create an atmosphere of inclusion that will permeate throughout the organization.

Walk and Talk

OBJECTIVE
• To build deeper connections with team members

Group Size
Partners
Materials
None
Time
5 to 8 minutes

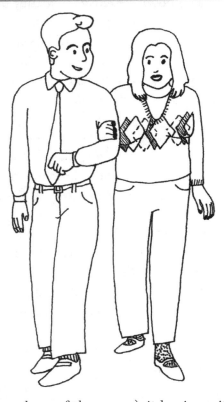

Procedure

There are significant differences between introverts and extroverts that can play out during an educational training program. In this book, we present a wide variety of opening activities that are suitable for many different situations. This activity, Walk and Talk, is one of the best ways to begin a program, especially for introverts. Instead of starting with a large group (which can be quite threatening for some members of the group), it begins with just two people taking a stroll and having a conversation.

Begin by inviting everyone to stand next to another person they have not yet met (or perhaps they know the least about) and link elbows with this person. Inform them that they are to take a three-minute stroll with their partner and while walking with this person, they are to find three things they have in common with each other. Encourage partners to go beyond visible things like the color of their clothing or similar footwear. For example, finding out they both like to read is a level-one connection.

Finding out they have both read the same book, or like the same author, or both received the same electronic reader for a present is a higher level of connection. Perhaps they both like Italian food, but by digging deeper discover that they enjoy the same restaurant or the same Italian dessert. It is this style of similarity that is the goal of this activity.

When people discover that they have something in common with others, it creates a unique bond. The love of pets, books, old movies, sporting events, TV shows, music, and food are all subjects that can create a sense of connection between people who enjoy these things.

When your participants have completed their walk and returned to the training area, invite them to share their most unique commonality with everyone in the group.

The activity continues until everyone has returned. At this point, the facilitator can ask if anyone would like to share one of the more unusual connections they had with their partner. Don't be surprised if you find these same partners chatting again later during a break or having lunch together. When people find common ground with others, it is typical for them to want to spend more time together.

Walk and Talk is an especially appropriate icebreaker for extremely large groups. Even with 100 or more people present, as long as there is available space, this activity provides a small-group interaction while hundreds of other pairs are completing the same activity in the same vicinity.

Tips

When it comes to creating a connection with others, a face-to-face encounter can seem almost confrontational. Walking side by side creates an atmosphere of connection, without continuous eye contact. Movement also stimulates the participants and brings energy to the conversation. By combining an ice-breaking activity with movement, participants not only make connections with their partners, they also arrive back at their starting location with high energy.

Author, teacher, trainer, and facilitator Dr. Chris Cavert once remarked about the students in his classroom, "The more they know about each other, the less likely they are to hurt each other!" At the time, Chris was teaching in a tough urban school environment near Dallas, Texas. His students were ethnically and culturally diverse. They dressed differently from each other. What they brought in their lunch boxes was different. Their language, life experiences, religions, and much more were incredibly diverse, so it was easy for the students to say, "Yeah, we're different from them." So Chris spent a few days at the beginning of each school year creating connections in his classroom. Other teachers often remarked, "How did you get so far in the curriculum when you spent the first three days of school just playing games?" So Chris informed them that he wasn't just playing games. "My students are connected," he said. "I don't have the same discipline problems in my classroom that you do, because my students help each other." Chris had successfully demonstrated the power of connection in a classroom setting, and continues that process in his training programs today.

The Big Question

Group Size

More than 10

Materials

The Big Question handout, pens

Time

10 minutes

Procedure

This is a great activity to "get the conversation started" among your attendees. It is also an ideal activity to begin a program when not everyone has yet arrived. You can begin the activity with available attendees, and when more people arrive, they can quickly create their own question and join the group.

Using the Big Question handout, each person writes a question. When meeting another member of the group, they read the question on their sheet and their partner answers it. Their partner then reads the question on their sheet, and the first person answers it. After both questions have been asked and answered, the partners exchange papers and find a new partner and begin the process again.

Here are a few interesting questions you can use for this activity:

- What movie have you seen more than once? Why?
- Which teacher in your life was your favorite? Why?
- What is one thing that you can do really well?
- What is the farthest you have ever been from home?
- What was the most helpful advice you were ever given?
- What is the best meal you have ever had in your whole life?

The Big Question

In the box below, write a question you could ask a fellow participant if you were to interview that person for a local radio talk show. For example, you might ask questions such as:

1. What was the most unusual job you have ever had?
2. What is the definition of a life well lived?
3. Who has been the most influential person in your life. Why?

When you have finished writing your question, take this paper to the center of the room, find a partner, ask that person your question (you do not need to write the answer down), and then your partner will ask you his or her question (you answer it). When you are both finished talking, trade papers with your partner. Then find a *new* partner, and ask that person your *new* question.

Write your question here:

The Big Answer

Group Size

More than 10

Materials

The Big Answer handout, pencils or pens

Time

10 minutes

Procedure

The best way to escape from a problem is to solve it.
—*Alan Saporta*

Chances are that every member of your audience is currently struggling with one or more work-related problems or challenges. If, during your training program, you can generate helpful suggestions, advice, or creative solutions for these problems, you will greatly assist your audience. The following technique is an ongoing way to encourage group problem solving, empathy, collaboration, and teamwork.

Using the one-page information sheet at the end of this activity description, encourage each person to select one of his or her current challenges and present it in the space provided. Next, you have a choice about how to proceed. You can formalize this activity by asking each person to mingle within the group soliciting answers to his or her question, or by taking a few minutes to uniformly pass each paper around the group for potential advice. You can also make this activity a bit less formal, and place each question page on a nearby table and invite the members of your audience to visit the table during breaks. The first technique allows for additional information to be shared during the discussion, while the second technique allows for anonymous input from the members of the audience.

It can be helpful to the members of your audience to frame the type of question you'd ideally like to see for this activity. For example, in a training program related to leadership, a question related to the role of leadership when the members of the team are dispersed in a dozen different countries could be valuable.

If even a single helpful answer is provided, your audience will view this activity as extremely valuable. In many cases, suggestions build not only upon the initial question itself but from other pieces of advice contributed during this activity.

The Big Answer

A problem is a chance for you to do your best.
—*Duke Ellington*

We all have questions, for which we are constantly looking for answers. Write your choice of question in the space below and let's see if we can help you generate some creative solutions, helpful suggestions, or at least some food for thought.

My question is:

_____

_____

_____

_____

_____

_____

For those of you receiving this page, your task is to carefully consider the question above, and write your best advice, answer, or comment in one of the spaces below. Feel free to include your name if you'd like, so that the author of the question can ask you more details about your reply if necessary.

_____

_____

_____

_____

_____

Story Stretch

Group Size
Any

Materials
A compilation of seven pieces of music

Time
10 to 15 minutes

Procedure

> A leader is one who knows the way, shows the way, and goes the way.
>
> —*John Maxwell*

Finding creative methods for energizing any group can be challenging. If you can add the opportunity to learn or practice a valuable skill, you can turn a simple energizer into a valuable teaching tool. Story Stretch has both of these elements: a simple group energizer and an opportunity to provide leadership to the group.

Begin by dividing a large group into smaller groups of 8 to 12 people. Instruct one person in each group to tell a story and add movements to that story, and the other members of the group to listen carefully and repeat the movements of the leader. Then, after a short time (typically less than a minute), the next person in line continues the story, again with movements repeated by the other members of the group.

It can be helpful to provide a theme for each group, such as "How I typically start my day" or "Things I want to do on my day off." Such themes not only bring out the energizer and leadership components to this activity but also add an element of creativity and occasionally theatrical performance and fun.

Discussion Questions

1. Were some leaders easier to follow than others? What did they do that made them a good leader?

2. In addition to movement and motion, did they communicate what they were going to do? Did they seem confident in their leadership? Did they make it fun?

3. If you had to do this activity again, what would you do differently the next time?

4. Which leader in your group would you like to follow again?

Raccoon Circle Games

OBJECTIVES
- To get to know the members of our team
- To set the climate for the training

Group Size

Any

Materials

One Raccoon Circle (described below) for every 5 to 6 participants

Time

10 to 20 minutes

Procedure

One of the most versatile training props (and one that should absolutely be in your training kit) is a collection of colorful 1-inch-wide (2.5 cm) tubular climbing webbing segments approximately 15 feet (4.6 m) long, known as Raccoon Circles. Over the years, adventure-based facilitators have been steadily adding to the number and variety of activities that can be presented with this simple piece of equipment, and now more than 200 activities are possible.

Here are a variety of opening activities and icebreakers for Raccoon Circle groups of five to six people. Why is a group size of five to six people an optimum number for Raccoon Circle activities? Well, the short answer is that if you keep icebreaker activities to a maximum duration of eight minutes each, you keep the energy level high for your participants. The first activity that follows, Wrapped Around My Finger, invites each member of the group to talk for approximately 60 to 90 seconds as the participant wraps the Raccoon Circle webbing around his or her finger. Five or six people, each talking for 60 to 90 seconds can complete this activity in about seven minutes.

In addition to these opening activities and icebreakers, you'll find additional Raccoon Circle activities (for such themes as problem solving, consensus building, and debriefing) in other sections of this book. You can also download an Internet edition of the Raccoon Circles activity guide for free at www.teamworkandteamplay.com/raccooncircles.html.

Wrapped Around My Finger This simple but powerful opening activity is a brilliant method for encouraging participants to provide a longer and more complete introduction for themselves. While some participants in any group may be less than confident while speaking in public, this activity provides a tactile task to be performed, which occupies the part of the brain that controls nervousness. By performing this task while speaking, most participants feel more comfortable and relaxed.

Begin with multiple unknotted Raccoon Circles, one for each small group of five to six participants. One person in each group begins by introducing him- or herself while wrapping the flat Raccoon Circle webbing around his or her index finger. The participant continues talking until he or she has completed wrapping the entire length of the Raccoon Circle around his or her finger.

The result is a significantly longer introduction with many more details than just the name, geographic location, and job function of the person speaking. This activity provides an opportunity for each participant to share their personal story with the other members of their small group.

Where Ya From, Where Ya Been? This opening activity was first created when Jim had a participant from Scotland in a training class. Another member of the group remarked that he didn't really understand where Scotland was located, and upon hearing this, the Scottish participant instructed the group to make a large map of the perimeter of England and Scotland using the knotted Raccoon Circle. He continued by pointing to various locations on the map, telling stories about where he was born or his family lived, places he had traveled to, favorite vacation spots, and other interesting and often historically significant locations.

After completing the geography lesson of the Scottish region, other members of the group wanted to tell their stories about where they were born or interesting places they had visited. Hence the title of this activity, Where Ya From, Where Ya Been?

Begin this activity with a knotted Raccoon Circle in groups of five to six participants. Each member of the group is invited to create the perimeter boundary of the city, county, state, or nation where they were born, or of an interesting location that they have recently visited. Other group members can be helpful in creating this geometry, even supplying elevation changes due to mountains and valleys. Group members frequently ask questions about each location, and occasionally provide additional commentary if they too have visited that location.

At a leadership conference we attended in Virginia a few years ago, one conference keynote presenter mentioned that there were three things that each of us uniquely owns: our name, our reputation, and our story. Where Ya From, Where Ya Been? gives participants the opportunity to tell their story.

Tips

Ecourage your participants to create the Raccoon Circle map of their location of interest while other group members are holding the Raccoon Circle in the air. This keeps connection between the members of the group, and helps them stay engaged during the story. Allowing participants to place the Raccoon Circle map on the floor or ground disconnects them from the task and turns a *participant* into a *spectator*.

Twice Around the Block While most icebreakers allow the speaker to be in complete control over the duration of his or her commentary, this activity gives the listeners that power.

Begin with a knotted Raccoon Circle in small groups of five to six people. To begin, have the team stand in a circle holding the Raccoon Circle in their hands. The single person nearest the knot of the Raccoon Circle lets go and begins sharing information about him- or herself while the other members of the group slowly pass the knot to the right (in a counterclockwise direction). When the knot reaches the person who is talking the first time (once around the block), this gives an indication that half of that person's time has been used. When the knot reaches this person a second time (twice around the block), that person's turn is over and the knot is passed to another person in the group.

It is common and playfully humorous for a group to occasionally speed up the movement of the knot (in the hopes of getting the person speaking to finish more quickly) or slowing down the movement of the knot to allow the person speaking to share even more details with the group. Some groups become so intrigued with the content of the information that they forget to pass the knot, or continue to listen long after the knot has traveled twice around the group.

My Lifeline Using an unknotted Raccoon Circle placed in a straight line on the floor, invite one person in each group to begin traveling along the line (with the members of their group in tow) while describing some of the major milestone events of that person's life. For example:

> "I was born in a small hospital in Ohio that housed both a hospital and a veterinary clinic, so the door you entered greatly determined the quality of care you were about to receive. I attended a small country elementary school where my grandmother was the school cook, which was very cool. After school, I attended a local college, received my engineering degree, and went to work for a large corporation in another state. Over the years, I've visited more than 20 countries, written nearly a dozen books, and received two U.S. patents for my inventions."

Now, at some point in this presentation, the speaker will reach the present day, but that person's life is not yet over. One of the great opportunities we can give to our participants is the gift of looking forward to the future. Upon reaching the present day along their lifeline, invite participants to tell their small group about some of the future hopes and dreams they have for their life, for example:

> "I've seen photographs of New Zealand, but I've never been south of the equator yet. Someday I'd like to visit there."

One of the unique features of this activity is that it invites members of each small group to travel together along the lifeline of the speaker. As Dr. Paul Dennison, author of *Brain Gym,* states, "Movement is the door to learning." This activity certainly keeps each small group in motion.

All My Life's a Circle The title of this Raccoon Circle activity comes from the classic song by Harry Chapin, and is similar to the previous Lifeline activity, except in a circular format rather than a straight line.

Place a knotted Raccoon Circle on the floor. The knot marks the beginning of the time scale, starting with the birth of the speaker. As the speaker moves around the circle telling some of the important events of that person's life, the other members of the group travel with them. Some speakers like to tell their entire story in a single revolution of the circle; others like to walk and talk, telling their story during multiple revolutions.

As in the Lifeline activity, the speaker eventually arrives at the present day, and then is encouraged to mention significant goals or dreams he or she is looking forward to in the future. After the first speaker is done, another member of the group can begin the process of sharing the story of his or her life as the rest of the group joins the speaker, moving around the circle.

The Goal Line The final Raccoon Circle activity in this section is a goal-setting opportunity rather than a traditional icebreaker. Stretch an initially unknotted Raccoon Circle into a straight line. Next, tie three overhand knots into the webbing, at the beginning, middle, and end. These knots represent the beginning, midpoint, and end of the program. Next, participants are asked to set goals for what they wish to accomplish for each of these three stages of the program.

"First, I'd like to grasp the basic definitions of the subject we are about to discuss. By the midpoint, I'd like to have a working knowledge of the subject, and hopefully by the end of the program, I'd like to have the ability to apply the principles in my own work environment."

By sharing the goals and expectations of each group member in a public format, all participants learn to set goals related to their experience. This activity can be initially performed at the beginning of the program, but then repeated at the mid- and end points, encouraging participants to do what they can to ensure they achieve the goals they have set for themselves.

Raccoon Circles are 15-foot- (4.6 meter) long segments of 1-inch- (2.54 cm) wide tubular climbing webbing. You can typically find webbing at stores that sell climbing gear and occasionally horse-tack shops. With this simple prop, you can lead more than 200 group activities (all of which can be found in *The Revised and Expanded Book of Raccoon Circles* by Tom Smith and Jim Cain, Kendall/Hunt Publishers). You can also download a free copy of the *Internet Guide to Raccoon Circles* at www.teamworkandteamplay.com/raccooncircles.html. For an even wider collection of team and community building activities, consider The Ropework & Ropeplay Kit, a durable backpack filled with a sufficient collection of ropes, webbing, cord and string to facilitate over 400 activities, available from Training Wheels, Inc. at www.training-wheels.com or 1-888-553-0147.

4

Team- and Community- Building Activities

When you're part of a team, you stand up for your teammates. Your loyalty is to them. You protect them through good and bad, because they'd do the same for you.

—Yogi Berra

Bobsled Team

OBJECTIVE

- To build teamwork and communication

Group Size

Any, split into teams of 4

Materials

None

Time

10 minutes

Procedure

In the world of athletic competition, few sports can surpass the teamwork required in bobsled team competition. The following activity will explore that level of teamwork and collaboration and incorporate elements of communication, coaching and mentoring, adapting to change, and community building, all in a high-energy environment. And best of all, this activity doesn't require any props, making it a perfect energizer and team-building activity for any size group.

To begin this activity, invite the members of your audience to create bobsled teams of four people. Teams with three or five members are fine, but four people is optimal.

A gold-medal-winning bobsled team is not only great at teamwork, but also in adapting to changing conditions. For this reason, coaches (facilitators) teach their bobsledders the following commands:

- Change: The participant (athlete) in the first position moves to the last position.
- Switch: The participants in positions two and three change places.
- Rotate: Every person individually turns 180 degrees and faces the opposite direction.

For the first level of competition in this activity, each bobsled team will be asked to complete an increasingly difficult series of commands: "Change. Rotate-Switch. Switch-Change-Switch. Change-Change-Change. Rotate-Switch-Change." At this point you are sure to observe some general confusion and occasionally some absolute chaos among your bobsled teams. If you ask which teams believe they are delivering championship-level performance, you might get a few raised hands. For the rest of the group, a bit more practice is probably warranted before more competition. At this point, invite each of your teams to practice independently and help each other be successful. Have them practice the change, switch, and rotate commands on their own, but be prepared to deliver a higher level of performance for

the next round of competition. This independent practice time is one of the best features of this activity and will be revisited during the reviewing process at the completion of the activity.

For the second level of competition, increase the energy of the activity by inviting each group to turn to their teammates and say, "We can do this!" Next, deliver a series of challenging commands to your audience: "Rotate-Change-Switch. Change-Change-Rotate-Change. Switch-Change-Switch-Rotate. Switch-Change-Rotate-Switch-Change." At this point, some of your teams are likely to be feeling pretty good. They've worked hard, practiced well, and are ready for the finals.

The final level of competition is not only the most challenging, but it involves one additional command. If the coach (facilitator) yells the phrase "Loose caboose!" everyone scatters from their present team and quickly collects three other people to form a new bobsled team of four people. The transitional chaos caused by this command is well worth the effort. By forming new teams, participants quickly learn how to respond to change and perform at their highest level, even with new teammates.

After informing teams of this new command, invite them to turn to their present teammates and say, "I think we can do this!" Ready? Here we go! Change-Change-Rotate-Switch. Switch-Rotate-Change-Rotate. Loose caboose! Change-Switch-Change-Rotate. Rotate-Switch-Rotate-Change. Loose caboose!"

As a debriefing discussion, ask each group what they would need to do so that they could perform any of these commands flawlessly. It is also a great idea to ask participants what happened in their group when someone made a mistake. Did the other members of the group perhaps give them a push in the right direction? A helpful push in the right direction from a colleague is a great opportunity to discuss mentoring and coaching in the workplace.

Discussion Questions

1. How did your original team perfect their performance during the independent practice time? How could this same process be used in the workplace?

2. When you switched teams, how well did the new team work together? What contributed to this?

3. How do we make sure each of our teammates is on the right track?

4. What does it take to build consistent communication?

Community Juggling

Group Size

Up to 20

Materials

Soft throwable objects, such as tennis balls, stuffed animals, yarn balls, beanbags, plastic fruit, or other hand-sized but lightweight objects. For a typical group size of 12 people, you'll need at least six objects.

Time

20 minutes

Procedure

Here is a perfect team activity for those groups that feel they are juggling too many tasks at one time. Community Juggling requires focus, attention to detail, communication, and teamwork.

The first task in Community Juggling is to create a random but established order for each object to be passed around the group. A tennis ball is a good choice to begin this process. Begin by inviting each person to hold both hands up in catching position and to lower both hands once they have caught and thrown the ball. This will help to identify participants who have not yet received and thrown the ball. Encourage each person to pass the ball to another person across the circle from them. Continue this process until everyone has caught and thrown the ball, and it returns to the first thrower. Then toss the ball again using this same pattern. Repetition is encouraged here so that group members clearly know their sending and receiving partners.

After establishing this order, begin juggling the tennis ball again, but this time include some additional objects as well. Continue adding more objects until the performance of the group falters, then discuss how the group might refine their technique to improve their performance.

After your group becomes proficient with the basic Community Juggling task, consider adding a few of these higher-level challenges.

Higher-Level Challenges
Thank You
During the initial round of this game, encourage participants to clearly say the name of the person they are passing to. This encourages name recognition and respect. After receiving an object, players should reply "Thank you" to the person throwing to them.

Size, Shape, and Texture
Depending on the collection of objects you initially use for this activity, some participants may be particularly challenged by certain objects due to their size, shape, weight, or other physical features. Consider allowing the group to replace some of these objects from a second collection of soft throwable objects.

Reverse
The original direction of the objects introduced above is considered the forward direction. When the facilitator says, "Reverse," each person now throws to the person who was previously throwing to him or her, thus reversing the direction. To return to the original direction, the facilitator should say, "Forward."

Zoom
This command requires that every person in the group moves to a new location within the circle, and then continues the task of throwing and receiving to exactly the same people as before this command was issued. To move the group again, the facilitator should say, "Zoom again." To return to the original configuration, the command "Un-zoom" should be used.

Gloves and Oven Mitts

To significantly increase the level of challenge to the group, inform them that new safety standards require participants to wear safety gloves for this activity. Then pass out an unusual collection of mismatched gloves, mittens, oven mitts, and other hand coverings and continue the game.

Multitasking

Print a page or two of a corporate mission statement or annual report, or copy a few pages from a recent book of interest to the organization you are training. As the juggling begins, pass these documents around and ask each person to read a line or two before passing it on to the next person. Each person still needs to support the team effort of juggling while performing this additional task.

Maximum Performance

Begin with multiple objects scattered around the members of the group. Using about half as many objects as there are participants is ideal. Next, invite the group to set a goal for how many objects will still be in play after each has been passed completely around the group, returning each item to its original position. Encourage the group to try several times to achieve their goal, leaving time between each attempt for discussion and improvement suggestions.

Personalization

Attach one piece of masking tape to each object being juggled by the group and invite individuals to write on the tape some of the things they are currently juggling in their professional lives.

Object-Specific Techniques

Incorporate several objects that have unique properties and then use these properties to further challenge your group. For example, instead of tossing a basketball, you can require that it be bounce-passed to the next person or that after catching it, each person must bounce it once before passing it on to the next person. An inspiring object might require a bit of inspiration to be passed along with it. A stuffed animal might be passed while making a typical sound that this animal would make.

Reviewing Possibilities

The experiential learning process incorporates elements of action, reflection, and application. For this particular activity, each of the experiential learning elements is clearly defined. The action is the passing of objects around the group. The reflection is the process by which the group discusses their performance in this task, and the application is the transference of capabilities in this activity to real-life situations that are similar in nature. Encourage your group to consider each of these three elements as they discuss their performance during this activity.

If you happen to incorporate some of the higher-level challenges, the reviewing process can include some of these themes: When focusing on the increasing number of objects being juggled, did you remember to call out the name of the person you were passing to, and did you remember to say thank you to the person that delivered the objects to you? Were some objects significantly more difficult to pass and receive successfully? When confronted with a changing environment filled with Reverse and Zoom commands, how did this group react? Were additional safety features, such as gloves, truly helpful in the performance of this task?

Discussion Questions

1. What things are you currently juggling in your professional lives?

2. Which things are essential *not* to drop?

3. Which things are most important?

4. How does teamwork help/hinder your process?

5. What can the team do to help the team members juggle more effectively?

Character Cards

Group Size

Multiple groups of 8 to 10

Materials

One set of 24 prelabeled large index cards for each group, masking tape or rope

Time

20 minutes

Procedure

Here is an energetic activity that can be used to teach almost anything! It is a very simple memory game sometimes referred to as the Match Game. The basic elements include just 24 index cards and a short piece of rope or tape to mark the starting line.

Begin by identifying a theme or subject you would like to explore during your next training program. Although character has been chosen for the example presented here, nearly any theme can be successfully presented in this fashion. For example, you could develop foreign language vocabulary skills by pairing an English word with a foreign language equivalent as the appropriate match. You could promote math skills by creating a match between an equation and the correct answer to that equation. Historical themes can be explored by matching a significant date in history and the event that happened on that date. For young audiences, you could provide two matching illustrations of the same object. For a corporate audience, you could identify 12 components of the employee health care program or 12 themes from the newest company mission statement.

Next, create 12 pairs of index cards (24 cards total) with your themes of choice clearly written in bold letters. You'll need one set of 24 cards for each group of 8 to 10 people. Shuffle these cards and place them facedown on a table in random order. About ten feet (3 m) away from each table, place a

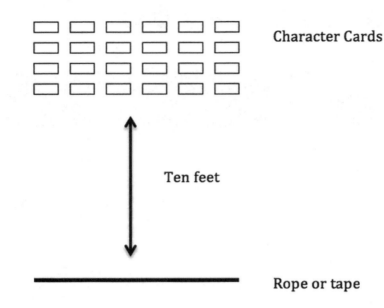

Character Cards

Ten feet

Rope or tape

short segment of rope or a piece of masking tape on the floor to act as the starting line.

Share these guidelines for this activity with each group:

One person from each group is allowed to approach the table and turn over any two cards. If these cards match, they are to be left on the table faceup. If they do not match (and after the rest of the group has seen each card), they must be placed facedown on the table in their original position. Then the next person approaches the table and again turns over any two cards. The first group to successfully turn over all 24 cards wins that round.

For the character theme presented here, the 12 cards include terms such as *honesty, integrity, teamwork, communication, respect, trust, tenacity, compassion, responsibility, equality, appreciating diversity,* and *positive attitude.* In some cases these cards are used with audiences with multiple language capabilities. For these cases, translations of words should be added to each card.

What is most fascinating about this simple activity is that the same cards that were used as props during the activity are also used as the debriefing tools after the activity. Here are three techniques for reviewing this activity.

Reviewing Techniques

1. With all cards faceup, instruct group members to circle around their table and choose one card that has a word on it that they feel is significant. Participants should hold this card so that others in the group can read the word or phrase they have selected. Next, invite each member of the group to share why he or she feels this word is significant.

This first round of reviewing allows each person in the group to choose a word that is most valuable to him or her, based upon individual preference.

2. After completing reviewing technique number one, ask participants to return their cards to the table. In this second round of reviewing, invite the group as a whole to select their top five choices for the cards with the most valuable words on them.

This second round goes beyond individual preferences and now assigns some value to each card, based upon the consensus of the group. The conversation that takes place in this round can be significant as different participants share their opinions related to the value of one character trait versus another.

3. In this final reviewing technique, ask each group to further refine their list of five valuable words down to just a single word. If you happen to have multiple groups for this activity, don't be surprised if different groups choose different words in this final round of reviewing.

Peteca

Group Size

Groups of 8 to 10

Materials

One peteca (described below) for each team

Time

20 minutes

Procedure

The game of peteca is traditionally associated with Brazil, yet variations of this game exist in nearly every culture of the world. It is a hand version of hacky sack, consisting of a weighted fabric base with several feathers, similar to a shuttlecock or badminton birdie, but hit with the hands instead of a paddle or racket. Some of the other popular names for this style of game include indiaca, featherball, funderbird, shuttlecock, and shuttlefeather. Some organizations have proposed that peteca should become one of the sports played in the Olympic games.

For the purpose of teaching, training, and facilitation, the game of peteca has a variety of potential teachable moments. The kinesthetic and physical movement associated with this activity can be used to increase the energy level of the audience after a particularly long presentation or meeting. It can be used as a team-building activity to see how well a group can work together, incorporating communication, timing, skill development, and teamwork. It can be used as a whole-brain learning activity or to explore changes in the workplace by requiring changes in the rules of the activity. There are so many ways to play that you may never need to play peteca the same way twice. It can also be presented as an entirely

playful and fun activity, with no additional need for a teachable moment beyond the connectedness possible when a small group plays together.

To begin, you'll need a peteca for each circle of eight to ten people. You can download the reference mentioned at the end of this activity with plans to make your own peteca, or you can substitute an inflated beach ball for all of the activities mentioned here. If you'd like to create a version of this activity that moves quite a bit slower (and wind is not a factor), consider using a large balloon.

To introduce the peteca to your audience, you won't need a long discussion of complicated instructions. Just say, "Everyone, hold your hands palms up like you were holding a tray. Your job is to keep this peteca in the air for a total of 21 hits, using just your hands. Ready? Go!"

In the first round, participants will be building skills playing a game that is probably new to them. You are likely to see the peteca fall to the ground several times during this round. After a few minutes, encourage your audience to discuss what is working and what is not working in their group. These kinds of discussions during play take this activity from a simple game to a valuable teaching tool. After the "what works/what doesn't" conversation, invite your audience to try again, but this time using only their nondominant hand.

Your audience's proficiency with this activity will increase with practice. Here is a list of several other variations we like to use with the peteca. The goal in each round is to achieve at least 21 hits without dropping the peteca.

Variations

1. Hit the peteca using either hand.
2. Hit the peteca using only the nondominant hand.
3. Hit the peteca using either hand but standing (balancing) only on one foot.
4. Hit the peteca using either hand, standing on two feet but clapping three times after each hit before being allowed to hit it again.
5. After hitting the peteca, participants must spin 360 degrees before hitting it again.
6. After hitting the peteca, participants must high-five someone before hitting it again.
7. A whole-brain learning variation in two parts: In part one, participants say their own name when they hit the peteca. In part two, participants must say the name of another member of their group when hitting the peteca, and nobody can say the same name twice in a row! This version requires both sides of the brain: a kinesthetic activity for one side, and a memory word recall for the other.
8. A second whole-brain learning variation. In part one, participants recite the alphabet (A through Z) instead of numbers. In part two, they must say the name of an animal that begins with that letter (aardvark, buffalo, cat, dog, elephant, etc.). For another version of part two, participants could say the name of a food beginning with the letters A through Z (apple, biscuits, cabbage, etc.).
9. As a final bonus round, challenge each group to play their favorite variation and attempt to reach the highest number of hits that they can.

Discussion Questions

1. What did you notice regarding teamwork as you progressed though the rounds?

2. What did it take to improve your performance?

3. What communication was most effective?

4. What are some team skills that were demonstrated?

Back Writing

Group Size

Any, split into groups of 5

Materials

For each group, five large index cards and a bold marker (pen); a flip chart with markers (for the facilitator)

Time

20 minutes

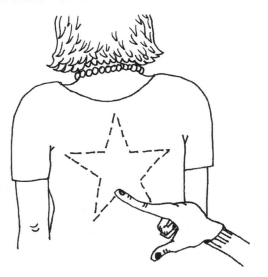

Procedure

> True interactivity is not about clicking on icons or downloading files, it's about encouraging communication.
> —*Edwin Schlossberg*

The ability to communicate effectively is a valuable life and corporate skill, especially in business environments where staff members often communicate via phone, fax, email, and text messages rather than face-to-face conversation. This activity will open the door to meaningful conversation about both effective and noneffective communication techniques.

Back Writing begins by forming groups of five participants seated in a straight line, with one person at the front and the remaining members of the group lined up behind them. An absolute minimum of four participants per line is recommended, and six participants per line is considered too many.

The challenge here is for the last person in each group (line) to view a drawing or sketch created by the facilitator and then transfer this information to the members of their group by drawing this image one time on the back of the person directly in front of them (using their index finger).

This person then passes the image he or she received to the next person in line, until it finally reaches the first person in line, who transfers this information onto an index card. Once all groups have finished, the facilitator reveals the original drawing to the group, and each group compares their version to the original.

As with many team activities, the value of this activity comes not just from participating, but in the discussion that follows, especially when it relates to the challenges of effectively communicating across great distances, time zones, languages, and cultures.

Begin with simple drawings of no more than a few elements. Here are examples of some of our favorites. Even at this level of simplicity, many groups cannot correctly transfer the image through four of their team members without significantly altering the final "message."

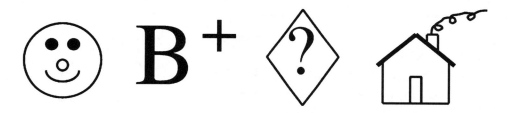

After each round, invite everyone to rotate to a new position within their group of five. This is easily accomplished if everyone moves forward one position and the first person in each line moves to the last position. This rotation allows each member of the group to experience all the different levels of communication (an important point that will become useful in the debriefing discussion later).

If you are not yet comfortable leading Back Writing, consider the following script to assist you in introducing and facilitating this activity. Begin the script once you have seated your participants into groups (lines) of five people each.

"Try to imagine just 50 years ago how folks in New York were able to communicate with folks in Los Angeles. What communication options did they have? There was of course the telephone, telegrams, U.S. mail, and a few private delivery companies. Now let's set the clock forward to the present day. In addition to those earlier ser-vices, we now have cell phones, fax machines, teleconferencing, voice messaging, texting, overnight delivery, and a host of new technolo-gies that help us connect. But even with these innovative technolo-gies, has communication really improved? Not really.

"Luckily, there is a new technology that we'll employ today. Raise your right hand and extend your index fin-ger. This is your new word processor. In a moment, I'll share an illustration with the members of your team in the back row. They will communicate the content of each illustration to you by drawing that picture on your back, just once. Why only once? Because when you hit 'Send' on email, it's gone! After you receive the illustration, you pass it along to the next person, and the next, until it finally reaches the front person, who then transfers this image to an index card. Then we'll check to see how much your copy looks like the original.

"Now, it is okay to tell your recipient, 'Okay, here it comes.' But it is not permitted to say, 'Hey, it's a tree.' In other words, only your index finger can be used to communicate the image, not your words."

Then begin with the first image. When the groups have completed their drawings, share the following information.

"It appears as though not all the details of our message have been successfully transmitted. Notice, however, that this method of com-munication is one-directional. But we know that good communica-tion is two-directional. Turn to the person behind you and tell that person two important components. First, what was good about what he or she did. Second, what that person could do to be even better. You might say, for example, 'Could you press a little harder?' or 'Could you draw a little slower?' Give them some feedback."

Continue rotating the members of each team with each illustration. When you have completed this activity (after five or so rounds), you can instruct participants to form circles within their group of five and invite each person to share a personal story of when communication may have fallen apart for him or her, or any personal insight related to effective or noneffective communication.

Discussion Questions

1. What did you do to improve your communication technique in this activity?

2. Did practice improve your performance?

3. How is this activity similar to the communication in your organization, department, classroom, or corporation?

4. What valuable insights can you take away from this experience?

5. If you were asked to advise a new employee how to effectively communicate within your organization, what insights would you offer them?

"Un-Blind" Square

Group Size

Up to 20 is optimal

Materials

One long rope (length depends on number of participants)

Time

20 minutes

Procedure

A significantly less frustrating variation of the Blind Square activity (which is traditionally accomplished with the entire team blindfolded), this activity provides a challenge while participants' eyes are open. For this task you'll need a long rope and a flat open space. As a rule of thumb, for ten participants the rope should be a minimum of 20 feet (6 m) long. For 50 participants, the rope should be at least 100 feet (30 m) long.

To begin this activity, invite participants standing around the perimeter to pick up the rope and securely fasten the ends of the rope together with a knot. From this time forward, participants are allowed to slide left or right from their present position, but they cannot let go of the rope or switch places with other members of the group.

Begin the first stage of this challenge by showing the first diagram (the square) to one person in the group and asking that person to lead the group in creating this shape with the rope. While this appears like a simple task, some leaders may simply instruct the other members of their team where to stand, rather than communicating (or sharing the vision) of making a square. No matter what technique is employed by the leader, evaluation of their leadership process can provide a valuable discussion at the end of this first stage.

For the second stage, repeat the process with another volunteer leader, using the second diagram (the double triangle, hourglass, or bow tie).

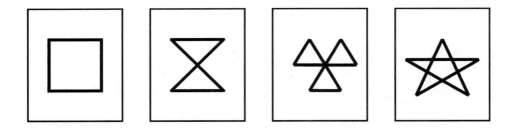

Again evaluate the effectiveness of leadership by discussing how the leader shared the vision of what was required, and the ability of the group to successfully complete the task.

Before stage three, ask the entire group to again form a circle with the rope, and then alter the leadership by showing everyone the illustration in the third diagram (the triple triangle or fallout shelter symbol). In this case, all members of the group have the vision of the pattern to be created. When completed, discussion can surround the concept of shared vision compared to leadership.

In stage four (the most difficult stage), invite the group to form a circle with the rope, and then show them the star diagram and ask them to reproduce this shape using the rope. While very challenging, this particular shape is indeed possible.

What is interesting in the fourth stage is that when asked, individuals can trace a simple star pattern with their fingers in less than a few seconds, yet completion of this task is likely to have required more than a few minutes. Why is that? Some participants may reply that the knot made the task more difficult. Then why didn't you untie the knot? This is an excellent metaphor for other "knots" that participants have created in the workplace that may be making things harder than they should be.

For a thorough explanation of each of the theories related to group development mentioned in this activity, see the book *Theories of Small Group Development* by Raye Kass.

Discussion Questions

1. How was leadership experienced during this activity? What did the leaders do?

2. Was everyone given the opportunity for their voice to be heard?

3. Were all members of the group equally engaged in the completion of the task?

4. Did the level of engagement change from stage to stage? Why?

5. How did "shared" vision affect the outcome in stage three?

6. What have you learned from this activity that you can use in your workplace?

Shoelaces

OBJECTIVE
- To use creative problem-solving, teamwork, and communication skills

Group Size
 Any
Materials
 Shoes with laces
Time
 10 to 20 minutes

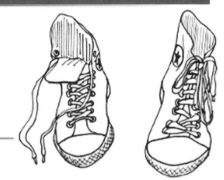

Procedure

Great things are not done by impulse, but by a series of small things brought together.
—*Vincent van Gogh*

As children, we learned how to tie our own shoelaces, but no one ever told us that it could be a team project! While this is probably one of the simplest activities in this book, it is filled with opportunities to explore a wide variety of useful skills, including communication, creative problem solving, coordination, collaboration, consensus, teamwork, and listening skills.

To begin, you'll need an audience where at least half of the group has shoes with laces. Invite everyone to find a partner so that every pair has at least one person with laces in his or her shoes. Next, have them untie the laces in just one shoe. The challenge is for both partners to work together, using just one hand each, to retie the laces on that shoe. This is not as easy as it may look.

When participants have completed the first-level challenge, invite them to try again using their other hand. Finally, for the master level, invite them to try completing this task with their eyes closed.

Discussion Questions

1. What was most challenging about this activity?

2. How did you work together to overcome those challenges?

3. What interpersonal skills were necessary to complete the task?

4. How can you relate this experience to work projects?

Bull Ring Candelabra

Group Size

18 to 36, split into three equal teams of 6 to 12

Materials

For each team: one "bull ring" made from 8 to 12 strings and a metal ring, tennis ball; for the entire group, a "candelabra" made from PVC tubes

Time

30 minutes

Procedure

When you are searching for the perfect final activity for your next training program, here is one that will not only leave your audience with a feeling of accomplishment, but leave them cheering as well.

The bull ring is one of the simplest team-building props ever invented. It consists of a metal ring with eight to twelve strings attached. This simple device can be used to transport a tennis ball, an egg, an ice cube, or a variety of other creative and challenging objects.

The basic task when using the bull ring is to transport a tennis ball or other similar object through a series of increasingly challenging obstacles, such as through a doorway or under a table. The addition of the candelabra

at the conclusion of this activity will invite several smaller groups to come together for one final large-group challenge.

To begin the Bull Ring Candelabra challenge, it is important to allow participants the opportunity to practice some basic skills before presenting them with the final substantial task. To that end, we recommend the following four stages of progression.

Stage One

Ask each group to lift their tennis ball into the air by using the bull ring, and then returning it to the original resting place (provided by a small plastic cone). Throughout the Bull Ring Candelabra activity, participants are asked to hold only the very ends of the strings. If the group drops the ball, there is no penalty here, just an opportunity to try again to improve their performance.

Stage Two

Ask each group to elevate their tennis ball, rotate their entire group halfway around (180 degrees), close one eye, and lower the tennis ball back down. This stage requires communication between participants as individual depth perception is eliminated.

Stage Three

All groups will need to work together as each group elevates their tennis ball, moves to a different location, and all groups lower their tennis ball at exactly the same time. What began as a single group is now growing to include all participants in this activity.

By this time, many groups will have experienced several failed attempts at transporting the tennis ball, and most will have developed the skills needed to be successful. Now it is time for the final challenge!

Stage Four

All groups begin the process of lifting and transporting their tennis ball using the bull ring device, but the final resting place is a uniquely designed PVC candelabra structure. The challenge is for *all* groups to place the tennis ball they are transporting on the candelabra at exactly the same time.

Using a variety of connectors and different lengths of half-inch PVC tubing, create a tower where several tennis balls can rest simultaneously. You'll need to create a stable base for the tower and rest positions that are at different heights. It is a good idea to create one more rest location than the total number of tennis balls being transported.

The total number of Bull Ring Candelabra participants should be limited to the number of strings present on three of the Bull Ring devices. This is generally between 24 and 36 participants. Greater numbers of participants and tennis balls are possible, but the length of the activity grows significantly with the addition of more participants.

Variations

For programs with limited space or a lack of PVC components, the four-stage challenge can be modified to include touching all of the available tennis balls together rather than placing them on the PVC candelabra. This challenge provides a similar level of problem solving and teamwork, though the candelabra version is a bit more dramatic when successfully completed.

Discussion Questions

1. What did it take to do this task successfully?
2. What contributed to the team's process improvement?
3. What challenges did you experience during the last round? How did you meet those challenges?
4. How can you relate this experience to the workplace?
5. What did you learn that would help you work more effectively together?

Alphabet Soup

OBJECTIVE
- To practice quality improvement and goal setting

Group Size
  5 to 20

Materials
  Large index cards, markers, one 50-foot
  rope, one 10-foot rope, flip chart

Time
  20 minutes

Procedure

Here is an activity that is sure to energize a group while exploring such important group skills as goal setting, creative problem solving, continuous improvement, reducing errors, leadership, and teamwork. This is one of a select few team-building activities that you can successfully repeat multiple times and sustain the active engagement and participation of your group. In fact, the energy of the group typically increases in each round as their performance continues to improve.

The name of this activity, Alphabet Soup, comes from the appearance of random letters floating in a circular bowl. You can create your own soup bowl with 26 index cards, printed with the letters A through Z, and 50 feet (15 m) of rope to create the bowl. You'll also need a shorter rope about 10

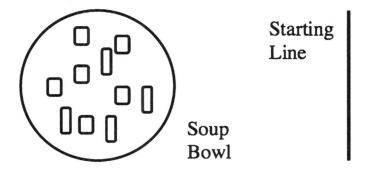

Starting
Line

Soup
Bowl

feet (3 m) long to use as a starting/finish line. This line is located about 30 feet (9 m) away from the circular bowl of letters.

The challenge in this activity is for a team to race from the starting line to the circle, touch all the cards in ascending order, and return back to their starting location as quickly and as error-free as possible. The basic rules for performing this task include:

1. The clock starts when the first person crosses the starting line and ends when the last person returns.
2. Cards must be touched in ascending order.
3. A five-second penalty is assessed for any of the following errors:
   - Having more than one person "in" the bowl at a time. This includes anyone reaching over the circular rope perimeter to point at a letter card.
   - Touching a letter card out of order.
   - Touching the perimeter rope of the soup bowl.
4. The total time for each round is a combination of the time required *plus* the total time penalties. A 60-second completion time plus ten errors (5 seconds per error) would create a total time of 110 seconds.
5. The cards, rope boundary, and starting/finish line positions are fixed and cannot be moved.

There are a variety of techniques that are possible for the successful and timely completion of this task. Some groups choose to have every participant touch at least one card. Some groups select one volunteer who touches all the cards in order, while other team members assist with verbal directions.

Before each round, invite teams to establish a time goal for themselves. When finished, compare this estimate to the actual performance. In addition to setting time goals, encourage teams to establish quality standards to minimize errors. As part of this "quality" management, encourage teams to inspect their own errors rather than using a facilitator to do so. This simple act places the responsibility for error accounting and reduction with the participants rather than with an outside observer.

If multiple groups are participating in this activity, allow each team to observe the performance of all groups. This technique will typically increase the inclusion of best practices from other groups, and produce an even more dramatic reduction in errors and time performance.

Keep track of both the performance time and error count for each group and record these on a flip chart or tally sheet. Include such information as group name, estimated completion time, actual completion time, total number of errors, and total time. This presentation typically assists groups in identifying whether they should focus on their performance time or on reducing errors, or both. The critical quantity in this activity is to minimize the difference between the estimated time and the total time (including errors) actually delivered by each team.

Teachers, trainers, and facilitators are inventive by nature and love to creatively alter team challenge activities. Alphabet Soup is a perfect example of an activity that can be easily modified to fit the needs of the audience. For example, the letter cards mentioned in the description above could be replaced with numbers instead. Or the cards could be replaced with cards identifying the various stages of a project that must be completed in order. For classrooms, conference rooms, and training spaces where floor space is limited, consider placing the cards on the wall or even the ceiling. For special needs audiences, including mobility concerns if the cards are placed on the floor, incorporate a touch stick to contact cards. This stick can be passed around the group as needed. For multicultural groups, incorporate different languages, number systems, alphabets, and other appropriate or perhaps culturally significant items.

Discussion Questions

1. How did you overcome communication challenges?

2. What did the team do to organize the process?

3. Did you have a plan? If so, how effective was the plan? Did it change? Why?

4. How can we use this experience to improve our work teams?

Snowflakes

Group Size

Any

Materials

One piece of paper for each participant

Time

5 minutes

Procedure

Provide each person with a piece of paper. Ask them to close their eyes, and then provide the following verbal instructions. "Please follow each of my instructions. You may not ask questions. Fold the paper in half and tear off the lower right corner. Fold the paper in half again and tear off the top right corner. Fold the paper in half again, and tear off a tiny piece of the lower left corner. Open your eyes and compare your snowflake to all the others."

Typically, each snowflake is different from each other. Even though the instructions were fairly simple, and everyone started with the same materials, the end result can be very different.

Discussion Questions

1. Did we have clear communication?
2. Was everyone listening?
3. Why do we have so many different results?
4. What are three things we can do to ensure our communication is received correctly?

Lighthouse

Group Size

Any

Materials

Various available props

Time

10 minutes

Procedure

Effective communication is essential in a high-performing work environment. But some environments are extremely challenging, especially when it comes to communication. This activity will explore such challenges and encourage groups to find communication techniques that will be successful, even in less-than-ideal environments.

In hazardous shipping waters, lighthouses provide helpful information to vessels. In this activity, half of the participants will act in the role of lighthouses and provide communication to help the ships in the area. The position of each lighthouse is fixed for the duration of the activity. The remaining participants will play the role of ships in the region. These players will voluntarily close their eyes for the duration of their passage, responding only to the voice commands of their lighthouse communicator. Underwater obstacles, flotsam (floating debris), and jetsam (discarded cargo) can be created using any available resources, such as other team-building props, books, chairs, and tables.

To begin this activity, each lighthouse is partnered with a single ship. The challenge will be for each lighthouse to communicate to their designated ship, helping them navigate the obstacle-filled shipping lane until they successfully reach the lighthouse location. This task is made slightly more difficult by the presence of other ships and lighthouses in the area, as well as communication channels filled with additional chatter.

After a few minutes of communication chaos, invite each lighthouse and corresponding ship to move to a location away from the shipping lanes and discuss how to improve this situation. After a few minutes of discussion, invite everyone to return to their original starting positions to try again.

Variations

In addition to navigating the obstacle-filled shipping lanes, lighthouses can also provide information to help ships pick up cargo along the way, or transfer cargo from one ship to another during the passage.

Although ships are asked to keep their eyes closed for the duration of the activity (creating dependence on the lighthouse for successful navigation), it is permissible for the ships to briefly open their eyes once during their journey. It is as if the fog in this region has temporarily lifted, albeit only for a brief moment.

Some of the obstacles floating within the playing space can potentially move during high tide or new obstacles might float into the path of an oncoming ship.

Once ships have reached the location of their lighthouse, invite partners to change roles and repeat the activity.

A No-Prop Version of This Activity

It is possible to conduct this activity with no additional props, using just the members of your audience. Begin by inviting the formation of three equal-sized groups. The members of the first group are the lighthouses and send information to the members of the second group, the ships. The members of the third group are the underwater obstacles, flotsam, and jetsam that make navigation difficult in this region. The challenge here is exactly the same as for the version above, for the lighthouses to successfully communicate to their ships and assist them as they move through the treacherous waters. Any ship making contact with one of the obstacles is initially compromised. A second contact and that ship is lost.

Discussion Questions

1. What did you find most confusing at the beginning of this activity?
2. Did you form a strategy with your partner, and did it work?
3. Were you conscious of others around you during the activity, or did you focus solely on your partner?
4. What technique did you use to reduce the amount of confusion during this activity?
5. What did you try that did not work?
6. What technique would you recommend to others?

Sunny Side Up

OBJECTIVE
- To build creative problem-solving skills and teamwork

Group Size

Multiple groups of 6 to 8

Materials

One 6-foot by 8-foot plastic tarp and one tennis ball for each team

Time

15 minutes

Procedure

Here is a challenging activity that never fails to engage and energize a group of participants. Sunny Side Up is a great activity for exploring the issues of teamwork, split-second timing, contributing to the success of a group, communication, and creative problem solving. Best of all, you can present this activity with simple, inexpensive props.

For each group of six to eight participants you'll need one tennis ball and a plastic tarp approximately 6 feet (1.8 m) by 8 feet (2.4 m). For convenience, other soft balls or even a stuffed toy animal can be substituted for the tennis ball, and a tablecloth, shower curtain, or bed sheet can replace the tarp.

The challenge of this activity is for a group to collectively hold the perimeter of the tarp, toss the tennis ball high into the air, turn over the tarp, and catch the ball on the way back down. To encourage advanced planning rather than a trial-and-error solution technique, invite each group to plan and practice without the ball until they have confidence they can successfully perform the task. Then inform them that they have just one chance to get it right.

To further challenge a group that has already successfully demonstrated their abilities, inform them that a high-performing work team can either catch the ball twice in a row, or can catch two balls at once. One work group even managed to flip their tarp *twice* before catching their tennis ball.

As a facilitator, you'll know when one of your teams has completed this task. Most teams will cheer loudly when they are successful. In addition, most teams will persevere until they are successful. Tenacity is a valuable team skill and this activity encourages it.

Finally, for the debriefing component of this activity, focus on transferring skills perfected in this challenge that can be applied in the workplace.

Discussion Questions

1. Are there any situations where you only have one opportunity to do the job right? Some folks would counter that you only have one chance to make a first impression!

2. Did every member of the group have the opportunity to contribute to the success of the entire team?

3. How many alternate techniques did the group consider?

4. How many of these were actually tried?

5. What are three valuable lessons from this activity?

Inside/Out

Group Size
6 to 8

Materials
Raccoon Circle for each team

Time
10 minutes

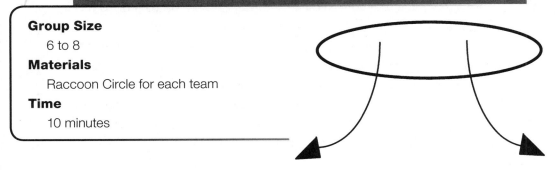

Procedure

Ethical behavior in the workplace is a valuable asset, but it is also a subject that can be challenging to present to an audience during a training session. As mentioned in Chapter 1 of this book, the activities in this book open the door to having meaningful conversations about things that matter. In this case, Inside/Out presents a challenge and some guidelines, which are often disregarded by participants. The discussion that follows can be both useful and profound.

In addition to the description of this activity, you'll also find useful resources for discussing ethical behavior in the workplace, together with a short but informative presentation on the various philosophies of ethics (did you know there was more than one kind?).

Begin by placing a knotted Raccoon Circle on the floor for each group of six to eight participants. Invite each group to step into the circle. The challenge is for the entire group to move from inside the circle to the outside by going underneath the Raccoon Circle, without anyone using their hands, arms, or shoulders.

To encourage the formation of a plan, rather than trial-and-error attempts, invite each group to walk away from their circle and hold an off-site planning meeting. When they have a plan, where every member of the group understands his or her responsibilities, ask them to return to their circle to carry out their plan. This process encourages each group to "plan their work" and then "work their plan."

After completing what they believe to be a simple task, most group members will feel that they followed the rules and successfully completed the task. As a check, ask if anyone in the group crawled on their hands and knees to exit the circle, or used their hands to hold up a leg or to balance against another person. The rules stated "without using your arms or shoulders or hands," but most people interpret this to mean that you cannot touch the Raccoon Circle with your arms or shoulders or hands. In this case, this ambiguity in interpretation is the invitation to discuss what ethical behavior means in the workplace. "How many people saw another person using their arms or shoulders or hands? How many said something about this? How can we expect our employees to follow the rules if we don't?"

As a further step, ask the group how you as an instructor could have been clearer in presenting the rules. It appeared that you were, by saying "without using your arms or shoulders or hands," but the behavior of the group didn't support this assumption. What would have made your instructions more clear? Is it enough to tell your employees the rules, or is more needed to ensure they get the message?

John Maxwell proposed one of the most unique definitions of leadership: A leader is one who knows the way, goes the way, and shows the way. What does this quotation have to say about ethical behavior in the workplace?

Additional Possibilities with Inside/Out

Once all groups have completed Inside/Out, invite them to perform the same challenge in reverse, Outside/In, going from the outside of the circle to the inside, again without using their arms or shoulders or hands. In this second attempt, do not remind them to plan first. Most groups will jump directly into the task without bothering to plan. This can be an interesting discussion question during the debriefing of this activity.

If a discussion on ethical behavior was conducted after the first round, a similar discussion can take place here to see if group members, now that they have been reminded about ethical behavior, are able to deliver a solution that is both successful and ethical.

A Brief Lesson in Ethics

Beyond the actual activity presented here, there is an opportunity to instruct your audience on the five traditional philosophies of ethics. For some members of your audience the fact that there are different kinds of ethics may be unfamiliar to them.

Begin by stating a simple definition of ethics. *Ethics* refers to standards of behavior that tell us how human beings ought to act in situations they encounter in their lives. These situations include not only business and professional encounters, but also situations involving families, friends, associates, and even total strangers.

It can also be helpful to identify what ethics are *not*. Ethics are not feelings, religion, science, or the legal system of laws and punishments. Ethics are not culturally accepted norms (everybody is doing it). So now the question becomes "If our ethics are not based upon feelings, religion, science, accepted social practices, or laws, what are they based upon?" The following presentation of five ethical philosophies should help to answer this question. These philosophies include rights, fairness or justice, utilitarian, virtue, and common good.

- **Rights.** Respecting and protecting the moral rights of those affected. This begins with the premise that all humans have rights and often incorporates the duty to respect the rights of others.
- **Fairness or Justice.** Equality for all, based upon the principles of fair treatment and justice for all.
- **Utilitarian.** Providing the most good or conversely the least amount of harm in a given situation. Based upon the consequences of an action, and optimizing the results of that action to do the greatest amount of good and the least amount of harm.
- **Virtue.** Comparing our actions to the "ideal" based upon character and values.
- **Common Good.** Respect and compassion for all. A community-based model of ethics suggesting the greatest good for the greatest number.

Even with such clearly stated ethical philosophies, there can still be problems. For example, we may not all agree on which definition of ethical behavior we wish to adhere to. We may not all agree on the same set of human rights or what constitutes "the common good." We may not even agree on which things are good and which are harmful.

Next, each of the different ethical philosophies does not answer the question "What is ethical?" in the same way. This alone produces significant discussions on the merits of each style.

So how can we make ethical decisions or create a valuable discussion about ethics in our teaching/training environment? One of the best starting points is to download and discuss the free paper, "Making Ethical Decisions," at www.sfjohnson.com/acad/ethics/Making_Ethical _Decisions.pdf. This comprehensive paper created by the Josephson Institute provides clear language about ethics, character, and ethical decision making, including an interesting section on rationalizations and other obstacles to ethical decision making.

One of the most prolific resources for ethical decision making is the Josephson Institute of Ethics (www.josephsoninsitute.org) founded by Michael Josephson. You can also explore ethics and other character issues and topics at the Character Counts website (www.charactercounts.org).

One of the classic activities for discussing values is Alligator River, presented by Sidney Simon, Leland Howe, and Howard Kirschenbaum in their book *Values Clarification: A Practical, Action-Directed Workbook*.

Discussion Questions

1. What did you observe during the activity?

2. Based on this experience, what did you learn about ethics?

3. How can you apply this in the workplace?

The Leadership Dance

OBJECTIVE
- To provide a kinesthetic leadership opportunity

Group Size

Any, in teams of 7

Materials

A compilation of seven pieces of music

Time

15 minutes

Procedure

There is nothing more notable in Socrates than that he found time, when he was an old man, to learn music and dancing, and thought it time well spent.

—*Michel de Montaigne*

The ability to react to a situation and provide leadership in that moment is a valuable skill. Michael Useem in his book *The Leadership Moment* describes nine such scenarios and points out the leadership lessons contained therein.

Preparing the members of your audience to take a leadership role can be a challenging task. Earlier in this book, a leadership opportunity was created during the warm-up activity Story Stretch. Here is a musical extension to that activity. Before you present this activity, you'll need a collection of seven appropriate pieces of music, with each song segment no more than one minute in length. You'll also need a large open space, without barriers or obstacles, to perform this activity.

Invite the members of your audience to form groups of seven people. Next, ask members of each group to count off, one through seven, and remember their number. Inform your audience that you are going to play several pieces of music, and that each member of the group will be given the opportunity to lead the group. The first piece of music will be led by person number one. The second piece of music is led by person number two, and so on.

A special benefit of this activity is that it not only provides an opportunity for exploring leadership but also energizes the members of your audience. This can be a valuable asset for full-day training programs, when group energy typically drops in the late afternoon.

Before you create your playlist of songs for the Leadership Dance, consider the following tips designed to help you increase your success with this activity. First, make sure to use music with a definite beat. Marching band and military songs work great. Next, use a diverse collection of music that reflects the diversity of your staff. Many libraries have a music collection that explores various types and styles of music (from classic rock to country to hip-hop to show tunes). You can even include television theme songs. If your training program (or corporation) has a theme, choose music that reinforces that theme. Third, be sure to limit the length of the song to no more than one minute in length. When you are leading a song that goes on and on, one minute can seem like a very long time! Finally, be sure that you have a music system that adequately amplifies the sound required, so that all participants can hear the music and the rhythm.

Discussion Questions

1. Consider which members of the group were the best leaders. What did they do that made them successful?
2. Did they appear confident in their duty? Did they appear to be enjoying the task? Did they show the way for others to follow?
3. How did they communicate what needed to be done? How did they motivate or inspire the other members of the group to follow them?
4. What leadership lessons can we take from this experience?

The Trust Drive

OBJECTIVE
- To foster trust, feedback, and relationship building

Group Size
Any

Materials
Script for the Trust Drive (provided)

Time
15 to 20 minutes

Procedure

In his book *The Speed of Trust*, Stephen M. R. Covey asserts that trust "is the one thing that changes everything." While there are a variety of activities that explore issues related to trust, the following is one of our favorites for demonstrating the beginning stages of trust formation.

The Trust Drive is a two-person driving scenario where one person takes the role of a non-sighted driver and the other person takes the role as the sighted GPS navigation system, providing information to the driver. The best location for this activity would be a flat, open space with no obstacles or fixed objects.

Begin by inviting each member of your audience to find a partner of similar height. Next, ask one person in each pair to take the role of the driver, standing in front, and the second person to take the role of the backseat driver, or GPS navigation system. The driver places his or her hands on an imaginary steering wheel (in the ten o'clock and two o'clock positions) and closes his or her eyes. This hands-up position creates an additional zone of safety in front of the driver. The backseat driver has the duty of keeping the blind driver informed about their surroundings, other drivers in the vicinity, and imaginary traffic signs (including speed limits).

After a minute or two, ask all drivers to stop, open their eyes, and provide some feedback to their sighted partners on two critical issues. First, what did their partner do that was good? And second, what could they do to improve and be even better?

After a brief feedback session, invite partners to switch roles and repeat the activity.

Consider using the following script for this activity.

Script for the Trust Drive

" Imagine that before today's training program, you received a call from [the company director's name here]. [He/she] asked you to stop by the store and pick up a few last-minute items for today's program, and has offered the use of [his/her] brand-new car. And it is a very cool car indeed. The bad news is that today's weather is very unusual. It is foggy. So foggy, in fact, that you (front-seat driver) can't see a thing. Close your eyes.

"Luckily, this car has GPS navigation, so backseat driver, you can see everything. Place your hands on the shoulders of the person in front of you, lean forward, and say this (and mean it), 'Don't worry, I'm going to take care of you!'

"Notice that the tone of your statement does quite a bit to help your front-seat driver either feel comfortable or not. This is not bumper cars (dodge 'em cars in the UK). This is not a demolition derby. Our goal today is zero contact with other drivers or fixed obstacles. And why do you want to be a great backseat driver? Because halfway through, when I say, 'Switch places!' your partner is going to remember just how good you were.

"Backseat driver, say to your front-seat partner, 'I've got your back! Start your engines. Off you go!'"

Throughout this activity, facilitators can observe the nature of each member of the group. Some backseat drivers are creative and playful. Some blind drivers are risk takers and fearless. Encourage good driving skills, proper use of signaling, appropriate driving speeds, and especially safe distances between drivers.

To debrief this particular activity, consider focusing on the nature of the trust-building process. For many participants, establishing physical trust with a partner can be the first step to building trust in other areas as well. We associate the ability to trust people in one endeavor, and automatically extend this trust to other interactions, thus making the Trust Drive a valuable activity for initially building trust within a group.

Discussion Questions

1. Did any groups have difficulty establishing trust?
2. Were there any traffic accidents (fender benders) that resulted in the loss of trust?
3. What did your backseat driver do that made him or her dependable or trustworthy?
4. What could you do to improve your ability to be trusted?

Magic Carpet

Group Size

Multiple groups of 8 to 10

Materials

One "magic carpet" (described below) for each team, paper, pens, masking tape, flip-chart paper

Time

15 minutes

Procedure

Here is another excellent example of how a simple activity can create a significant teachable moment for your next training program. In this collection of Magic Carpet activities, the members of your audience will be encouraged to set goals, discuss barriers to reaching these goals, creatively solve a problem with limited resources, work together as a team, and celebrate their eventual success.

The basic challenge is for teams of eight to ten people to turn over their magic carpet without lifting people up and without touching the floor surrounding their magic carpet. The actual magic carpets used in this activity can be made from plastic tarps, blankets, tablecloths, or shower curtains. Each Magic Carpet team should be placed in close proximity to other teams.

Magic Carpet with Goal Setting

Here is a technique for using the Magic Carpet initiative to include a goal-setting opportunity for each member of the group. Place several magic carpets in close proximity to each other, and ask eight to ten participants to stand around the perimeter of each carpet. Provide a piece of masking tape to each person and several ink (not felt marker) pens. Invite each person to write a job-related goal he or she has on this piece of masking tape, and firmly attach it to the top surface of the magic carpet. When all team members have completed this assignment, encourage them to voice their goal to the other members in their group.

Next, turn over each magic carpet, and again provide participants with masking tape and pens. Invite each participant to write down any barriers they might see to reaching the goal they specified on the other side of the magic carpet. These can include budgetary limitations, time restrictions, resource issues, and other significant and real obstacles to the successful attainment of the original goal. Encourage everyone to share the barriers they identified.

Now ask everyone to step onto the magic carpet (which is now showing the barrier side). The challenge is for this group as a whole to reach their goals that are on the other side by turning over the carpet, without lifting anyone up and without touching the floor in the space near each carpet.

Just as in the basic version of the Magic Carpet initiative presented above, most groups will attempt to turn over their carpets on their own. While a few groups may actually succeed with this technique, there is a better approach. By creatively using available resources (and looking for a win-win solution), several groups will no doubt help each other reach their goals.

At the completion of this activity, have two flip-chart pages ready with the words *goals* on one page and *barriers* on the other. Invite each participant to place his or her goal and barrier tape on these pages. Keep these signs in the training area for future reference and discussion opportunities.

Prior to introducing the Magic Carpet challenge to a group, I like to create a bit of competition within the group by presenting an activity known as Grand Prix Racing. You can download for free the Internet version of over a dozen Raccoon Circle activities, including Grand Prix Racing, at www.teamworkandteamplay.com/resources.html. The competitive nature of Grand Prix Racing places most participants in a noncollaborative frame of mind. After completing several rounds of racing, I ask each team to stand completely on their magic carpet. Next I instruct them to turn over their carpets without lifting anyone up and without touching the ground. I finish by saying six words that almost guarantee that these groups will compete rather than collaborate: "Let's see which team finishes first!"

Groups typically struggle at this point to perform the task by themselves. This is an opportunity to stop an activity in the middle and create a discussion with the group. When asked what the two rules are, many groups will respond, "Without lifting anyone up and without stepping off the magic carpet." You can then respond, "But I didn't say you couldn't step off. All I said was that you couldn't touch the ground. When in this activity did you become several separate teams instead of one single team?" Most groups will reflect on the competitive nature of the previous activity and realize that they reacted to a prior situation instead of working toward building a team. At this point, ask each Magic Carpet team to begin again, and this time look around for additional resources that can help them accomplish this task successfully.

Discussion Questions

1. What barriers did you overcome to reach your goals?
2. What was required to successfully reach your goals?
3. Was a plan necessary?
4. Did you use all available resources? Why or why not?
5. What did you learn that you can apply to goal attainment in the workplace?

Engineering 101

OBJECTIVE
- To explore communication and creativity

Group Size
Multiple groups of 5 to 6

Materials
One construction set (described below) for each group

Time
20 minutes

Procedure

Here is a challenge that explores creativity, communication, and teamwork and incorporates a fast-paced engineering development and manufacturing environment.

To begin this activity, divide your audience into multiple groups of five to six people per group. Pair each group together with another group to form one project team. The first group in each project team will use the building materials to create a single interconnected product using all of the pieces available. The second group in this same project team will be tasked with reproducing the product designed by the first team using an identical collection of building materials. A recommendation for building materials can be found near the end of this activity. The ideal construction set for this activity should include a variety of approximately 20 pieces.

The two groups in each project team should be located a sufficient distance away from each other so that members of each group cannot see what the other group has created. A location midway between each group will be the "conference room" location, where all joint discussions will take place.

Initially, the first group is given four minutes to create one product using all of the available pieces of construction materials. The only requirement is that all pieces must be firmly connected to each other. During this same time, the second group can prepare their workspace and familiarize themselves with the available building materials. After the completion of this initial task, each group will send one member to the central conference room location for a one-minute-long discussion about the project. This is the ideal time for each group to discuss, piece by piece, what the first group has created and how the second group can duplicate this same product.

After each meeting, group members will return to their same group and have another minute to prepare for the next meeting. This series of one-minute joint meetings followed by one minute of building and planning continues for six rounds (allowing each person in each group to be part of a single discussion meeting). At the discretion of the facilitator, the final meeting can be two minutes in length.

After the final joint meeting, the second group has two final minutes to complete their construction and then both groups bring their products to the central conference room location for comparison. In most cases, the original product design and the duplicate are generally similar; however, depending on the building materials chosen, some small variations can occur. Each of these small variations is an opportunity for discussion and a potential teachable moment.

Recommended Building Materials

Nearly any kind of construction sets, wooden blocks, erector sets, or building toys can be used, but some are better suited to the task than others. Building blocks that are all similar in size and shape are a bit too regular (and easy) for this task. Irregular angles, odd shapes, unique colors, and other unusual differences in the construction pieces make for a more challenging and fun activity. Just be sure that the sets of building materials for the design group and the replication group are identical in every respect (color, number of parts, shapes, textures, part size, etc.).

Discussion Questions

1. What challenges did you face during the activity? What did you do to overcome these challenges?

2. In what way were your challenges similar to those at work?

3. If you had to do this again, what would you do differently?

Changing Places

Group Size

6 to 8

Materials

Paper, pens

Time

30 minutes

Procedure

When you're through changing, you're through.
—*Bruce Barton*

Puzzles make for interesting challenges, and some of the best puzzles can be modified in size so that more than one person can find themselves not only as part of the puzzle itself but also as a significant part of the solution process. The following class of puzzles is historically known as *shunting puzzles*, from the process of reordering train cars. In tabletop fashion, counters or coins were often used in creating these puzzles. For the purpose of active training, we'll incorporate people to reproduce these unique and engaging puzzles. Best of all, the solution to these puzzles will require the engagement and creativity of each member of the team, not just a single individual.

For each of the human-size puzzles presented in this section, you can use pieces of paper, cardboard, index cards, paper plates, wood blocks, plastic lids, placemats, or carpet squares as place markers or stepping-stones.

A Change of Management

The first challenge in this section illustrates both a classic puzzle and a variety of techniques that you can incorporate to additionally challenge a group and create more teachable moments.

Begin with six participants standing as shown on seven pieces of paper that serve as place markers or stepping-stones for this puzzle challenge. The middle location is vacant at the start and finish of the activity but can be temporarily occupied throughout the relocation process.

Tell the group:

"The management team of your division has done such an outstanding job recently that you have been invited to review the processes of another nearby division. Part of this review requires your team of three managers to change places with the three managers of the other division. The relocation process you've been asked to follow has the following standard regulations:

1. The task is to have the team on the left change places with the team on the right.
2. You can move forward into any open space. You cannot move backward.
3. You can jump over (around) a member of the opposite team, into any open space, but you cannot jump or pass a member of your own team.
4. If you reach a position from which you cannot move forward, and the system becomes 'locked,' the entire group must return to the beginning and try again.
5. There is no penalty for trial-and-error solutions, but try to be as efficient as possible and learn from any mistakes that happen.
6. As you learn the process of relocation, record any specific recommendations you experience that could assist a future group in performing this task successfully."

Through a series of trial-and-error attempts, participants eventually discover a process that will enable the successful relocation of each team. For the above case, with three participants on each team, it will take a minimum of 15 moves to successfully complete the task. To additionally challenge a group, try some of the following variations:

1. Ask the group to complete the task again, but this time without talking.
2. Ask the group to complete the task again, but this time without breathing! In other words, ask them to be so efficient that they can complete the task before anyone in the group needs to take another breath (this is about 20 seconds for most groups).
3. Alter the number of members in the group from three people on each side to four people on each side. You can also consider the case where one side has one more or one fewer person than the other—for which a solution is still possible. Three team members per side require 15 moves, four team members require 24 moves, and five team members per side require 35 moves.
4. For a future group, do not provide the rules but rather invite them to discover the regulations for relocation by trying various things and learning what is permissible and what is not.
5. Alter the geometry of the challenge, as shown in the following variations.

Changing the World Order

In this variation of the puzzle presented above, six participants are numbered in ascending order and initially placed as shown and then challenged to reorder themselves in descending order to the final configuration shown. It can be helpful to place a number on each participant, using a name tag or adhesive label. Participants can move forward or backward, can move into any open space, and may jump over (or around) a single teammate as needed. After completing this version with six participants, try it with seven.

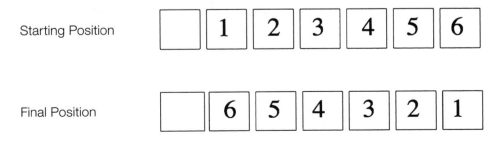

Starting Position   1 2 3 4 5 6

Final Position   6 5 4 3 2 1

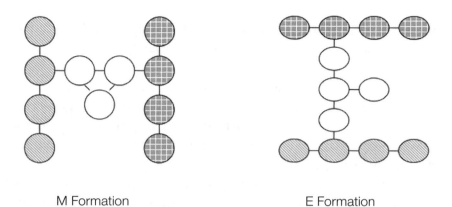

M Formation   E Formation

Changing Places with New Geometry

Here are similar people-moving activities in slightly different formats. In both the M and E formations (shown above), the task is for each group of four to trade places with the other team of four on the opposite side of the puzzle space. Participants will need tenacity and perseverance in order to complete these challenges. In these puzzles, teams alternate movements and participants can slide into any open space, but no jumping is allowed.

The final variation of people-moving challenges in this section comes from the three configurations that follow. You can choose the size of puzzle

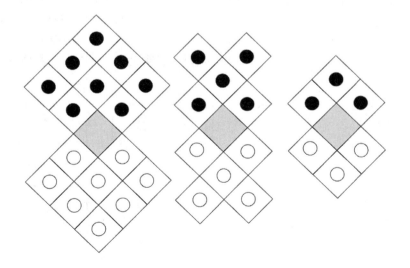

that most adequately engages the number of participants in your program, in this case 16, 10, or 6 participants.

In each configuration, teams are asked to change places. Each move consists of sliding into any open position or jumping over (around) any other person. Team members are allowed to jump around anyone, including members of their own team. Once a group has successfully completed this task, invite them to try again, without making a single mistake, or attempting to minimize the total amount of time needed to complete the task.

Teachable Moments

Each of the puzzles presented here can be used to encourage trial-and-error solutions, learning and adapting from our mistakes. You can further encourage the concept of an experimental laboratory by offering a group ten minutes to make as many attempts (and mistakes) as possible before a demonstration of their hopefully successful technique. The concepts of "failing forward," "learning from our mistakes," and even "becoming better as a result of trying" are well demonstrated by using these puzzles. You can learn more about this concept by reading *Failing Forward: Turning Mistakes into Stepping Stones for Success* by John C. Maxwell, or the more recent *Adapt: Why Success Always Starts with Failure* by Tim Harford.

In addition to the problem-solving teachable moments here, there is also the opportunity to explore the topic of leadership. Leadership is a bit easier when the people you are leading also know where they are going and how to get there. The puzzles in this section encourage self-direction and the need for group vision and execution. Individual competency and accountability are also necessary. Themes of recovering from failure, learning from mistakes, continuous improvement, and adapting to new challenges can also be presented as teachable moments here.

In some cases, solving these puzzles as tabletop amusements is substantially easier than trying to find a solution when people are used instead of coins. Factors such as motivation, encouragement, mentoring, leadership, communication, and teamwork are involved when additional people are involved, making the process a bit more complicated but significantly more like a traditional work environment.

Tips

Thousands of historical publications, including many more than 100 years old, have been scanned page-for-page and placed in digital form at www.archive.org. These significant publications, including the 1917 Henry Ernest Dudeney book *Amusements in Mathematics*, are filled with hundreds of puzzles, many of which are easily adapted for teaching, training, and facilitating groups. Best of all, these digital files are produced in a variety of formats for electronic reading devices and computers, and they are available free of charge.

Discussion Questions

1. How did you get the perspective necessary to solve the problem?

2. During this activity, did some participants become disengaged? Why?

3. Describe the content and quality of communication between those standing in different spots.

4. What can we do to encourage a higher level of engagement at work?

5. What can we do to ensure clear communication?

Zoom

Group Size
Up to 30

Materials
One *Zoom* or *Re-Zoom* book

Time
20 to 30 minutes

ZOOM

Procedure

Here is an excellent communication activity that is simple to create and facilitate. Begin by purchasing a copy of *Zoom* or *Re-Zoom* by Istvan Banyai. You'll find that each of these books contains a series of about 30 illustrations similar to a series of photographs seen through a camera with a zoom lens. The back of each page is blank.

In advance of the activity, remove the binding and covers from the book so that only the individual pages with illustrations remain. For durability, you may wish to laminate these individual pages. Shuffle the pages of the book and pass out one page to each person in the group. Inform them that they are allowed to discuss the content of the picture they are holding, but they cannot allow anyone else to view their picture.

The challenge for the group is for each person to communicate the content of the page he or she is holding and to ultimately place each person in the correct position according to the content of his or her picture. Informing your audience that the title of the book is *Zoom* may help them make sense of proper order for these illustrations.

For groups of 30 participants, this activity can easily take 30 minutes to complete. To shorten the length of time necessary, consider one of the following variations:

1. Allow one person to circulate among the members of the group, occasionally viewing the content of their pages and suggesting to other members of the group that they should meet (i.e., people with a similar content in their illustration).
2. Place a few cards, such as the first, last, and middle cards, in clear view of the group and inform them that each of their cards fits among these three cards.
3. For a single period of 15 seconds, allow each person to turn over his or her card so that others may see it.

We recommend the book *Zoom* as the first book you should use for this activity. For repeat audiences or for a higher level of challenge, *Re-Zoom* is a bit more difficult, as the changes between each illustration are a bit larger in *Re-Zoom*.

Zoom
ISBN 0-14-055774-1

Re-Zoom
ISBN 0-14-055694-X

This activity requires clear communication around sequential photographs. A more linguistic version of a similar activity is also contained in this book, entitled Active Quotations.

Discussion Questions

1. How did you organize your information?
2. Was a leader necessary?
3. How would you describe your problem-solving process?
4. Did your plan change? If so, why?
5. What was the level of engagement of the team members? What are some reasons for this?

A Knot Between Us

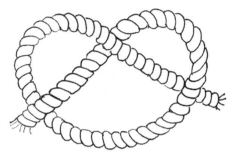

Group Size

6 to 20

Materials

One 30-foot rope; one 6-foot rope for every two participants; one 3-foot piece of tubular webbing for each participant; one Raccoon Circle

Time

10 to 30 minutes

Procedure

Here is a collection of knot-related team- and community-building activities that you can include in your next program. All you need are a few pieces of rope and tubular webbing.

Knot Right Now

For this activity, you'll need a 30-foot-long (9 m) piece of rope for each group of eight participants. To begin this activity, place the rope on the floor and then instruct each member of the group to grasp the rope with both hands. The location of their right hand on the rope must stay in this position for the duration of the activity, but the left hand is allowed to move as necessary. The challenge is for each group to tie a single overhand knot in the rope.

Solutions for this challenge range from the difficult but possible task of creating the knot near the middle of the rope, to tying the knot at one end of the rope.

Prior to beginning this activity, it can be useful to have the members of your audience practice knot tying on short segments of rope so that each person is well acquainted with a variety of knots. In addition to the overhand knot used here, you can also specify other common and familiar knots.

Tree of Knots

This variation of the previous activity uses the same equipment but includes a tree, column, or pole as the anchor point for this knot-tying challenge.

The basic task here is for a group to tie a square knot on the front side of the tree. Participants are told that where they place their right hand must stay connected at that point for the duration of the activity, but the left hand is allowed to move as needed.

The additional complexity of this knot compared to the overhand knot above typically requires some leadership from within the group. The location of this knot, against the tree, also requires nearly every person in the group to be kinesthetically engaged throughout the activity.

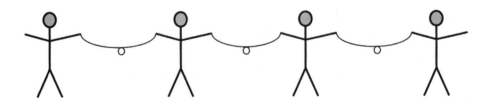

Tie the Knot/Untie the Knot

For these two activities, you'll need 6-foot-long (2 m) segments of rope between every participant. In groups of four to six participants standing in a straight line, group members work to create an overhand knot in each of the ropes.

The second version of this activity is to untie the knot in each rope. In each case, participants are asked to firmly grasp each end of the rope they control for the duration of the activity.

Knot on the Phone

This activity combines rope knotting, leadership, and communication skills in an engaging format. Begin by asking for a volunteer leader. Take this person aside and instruct him or her how to tie a water knot in a piece of flat tubular webbing. The Raccoon Circles mentioned in this book are exactly this kind of material.

Next, create a metaphorical situation and inform the volunteer leader that part of his or her job assignment will be to assist the "help desk" team with customer questions related to knot tying. Then invite the volunteer leader to instruct the remaining members of the group in successfully tying a water knot. Requiring that only verbal communication can exist between the leader and the members of the team increases the complexity of this task. The help desk system does not currently allow for visual information to be shared.

For this activity, you'll need one piece of flat tubular webbing about 3 feet (1 m) in length (available at many outdoor stores) per person. Next, review the following procedure for tying a water knot, prior to sharing with the volunteer leader in each group.

Tying the Water Knot

With tubular webbing it is often necessary to form a circle or loop. While a variety of knots can be used, the water knot is one of the strongest and best. The water knot is so named because river rafting guides use such a knot with flat webbing so that even when wet, the knot can easily be removed. Shown below is a simple technique for successfully tying a water knot.

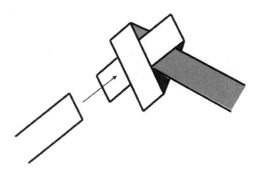

1. Start by tying a simple (but loose) overhand knot **(Fig. 1)** in one end of the flat webbing, with a short tail (less than 2 inches [5 cm] long). This first knot is known as the "teacher knot."

2. Next, travel the length of the webbing, untwisting the webbing as you go, and hold the opposite end of the webbing. This end is the "student end" of

the webbing. The student does everything the teacher does; the student just happens to do it backward. This means that first, the student looks directly at the teacher (each tail end of the webbing nearly

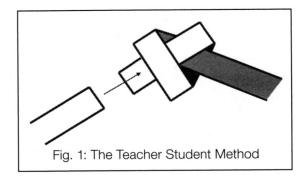

Fig. 1: The Teacher Student Method

touches). Next, the student "doubles" the teacher by following the same path as the teacher backward. This involves following the webbing, and finally tucking the student end of the webbing into the teacher knot, leaving about a 1- or 2-inch-long [2.5 or 5 cm] tail.

3. Now pull the opposite sides of the knot to secure it **(Fig. 2)**.

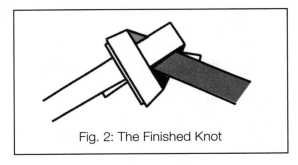

Fig. 2: The Finished Knot

5

Puzzles and Games with Teachable Moments

We are continually faced with a series of great opportunities brilliantly disguised as insoluble problems.

—R. Buckminster Fuller

Active Quotations

Group Size

Any

Materials

Quotations, one index card per participant, marker

Time

10 to 15 minutes

Procedure

The road to wisdom? Well, it's plain and simple to express: err and err and err again, but less and less and less.

—*Piet Hein*

Quotations are an inspirational way of introducing content to your training audience. You can include them within your course materials, print them and place them on the walls of your training room, and even use them in your pretraining information. But such presentations are passive at best, and there is little guarantee that this style of presentation will make a memorable impact on your participants. To ensure that your audience remembers the content of quotations you choose to include in your program, they need to actively engage with these words of wisdom in a manner that will move the quotations from short-term memory into long-term memory.

As an example, consider the last time someone told you a telephone number or a long website address. If you were not able to write this information down immediately, chances are that you were not able to retain it in your memory. The key to moving information from short-term to long-term memory is to manipulate that information for at least 20 seconds. That is why on some radio commercials, sponsors give their telephone number multiple times (hoping to accumulate at least 20 seconds of interaction). If you sincerely wish for your audience to remember inspirational quotations, mission statements, vision statements, and other important messages, try the following technique for increasing the duration of their interactions with this information.

To begin, find a printed or online source for inspirational quotations, such as *12,000 Inspirational Quotations* by Frank S. Mead or www .quotationspage.com, which has a searchable database of quotes. Select a suitable quotation. Next, using multiple index cards, transpose this quotation, using as many cards as you have participants in your program (use one card for each person). Be sure to print words in large letters that will be visible when viewed at a distance by other members of the group. It is helpful if most cards have more than a single word per card. For large audiences, you may wish to choose a quotation that has multiple sentences.

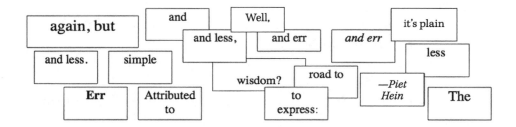

Then shuffle the cards and pass one out to each member of the group. Ask them to hold the cards face out, so that others can see the word(s) they have. The challenge is for the group to place the cards in the correct order so that the original quotation is revealed.

Here are a few hints to improve the quality of this activity. First, make sure each person has a card. Participant engagement goes up when each person has a card. Second, encourage participants not to give up their cards. Some groups may choose to place their cards on a table instead of in the hands of team members. When this happens, participants often become spectators, and only a few are actively engaged in the problem-solving process. When each participant has a card in his or her possession, each person remains a vital piece of the whole. Third, the facilitator can provide some hints to assist the group if they request it. For example, they can help place a single person and his or her card in the correct location, or they can tell which two cards go together. It is important for the facilitator (who knows the correct order of the quotation cards) to only provide hints, not the solution, so that the group can take the responsibility for finding the solution themselves.

For groups with multiple language skills, consider a quotation in a foreign language. Now instead of a minority of people speaking a different language from the remainder of the group, they become valuable assets for their language skills and leaders in this activity because of their ability to translate the message.

When the group has completed the task, ask participants specific questions about their problem-solving process, for example:

- How did you know where you should stand?
- Did you choose the location, or were you asked to stand there by another person?
- Was there a breakthrough moment for the group?
- Who provided leadership in completing this task?
- Did anyone offer advice on the solution for this problem that was disregarded by the group?
- What skills have you learned here that you can use in the workplace?
- How do you decode messages from management, or feedback from your customers?
- How do we make sure that we hear every voice in our group, especially the ones that are trying to help us move forward in the right direction?

Finally, ask the group to turn their cards over, hiding the words. Now ask them what the quote is. Chances are that most of them will be able to articulate the exact quotation, simply because their efforts created sufficient time to move this information from short-term into long-term memory. You can test this theory by asking them the quote a short time after this activity.

If you prefer a picture version of this activity rather than a text version, see the activity Zoom in this book. This communication activity challenges a group to place pictures that tell a story in the correct order.

Variations

In addition to inspirational quotations, there are other significant messages that can be utilized for this activity, including mission statements, vision statements, codes of ethics, personal credos, organizational pledges, corporate value statements, and other concise messages of importance.

As an example, to communicate their new corporate mission statement to their sales force, one organization chose to write all the words from their mission statement on index cards, but also added some additional words that were considered but not chosen by their board for inclusion. By re-creating the lengthy and difficult process of creating the mission statement in just a few minutes with their sales team, they were able to answer questions about various choices made during the process and engage their sales team in creating the same mission statement themselves. This was a valuable activity that ensured each sales-force member could articulate the mission statement word for word and understand why these specific words were chosen.

The Missing Link

OBJECTIVE
- To build consensus and practice listening

Group Size
Up to 30

Materials
Two ropes or Raccoon Circles (described below)

Time
10 minutes

Procedure

When it comes to identifying the most essential elements of a high-performing work group, the ability to reach agreement is certainly of great value. Here is an activity that explores two components of achieving consensus within a group: listening and influence.

The challenge of the Missing Link is for individual members of a group to decide for themselves whether two ropes are linked or unlinked and then influence the other members of the group so that consensus can be achieved. This challenge is made more difficult by presenting the ropes to the group in such a manner that it is not immediately clear whether they are linked or unlinked. In the process of trying to influence the final decision, group members are exposed to a variety of problem-solving techniques, opinions, beliefs, and occasionally erroneous thinking processes that may or may not lead to consensus. In many ways this particular challenge is similar to any typical project that requires consensus in the business world.

To begin this activity, the facilitator places two different-colored rope loops together. These two ropes can be linked together like the links in a chain or can be unlinked but simply lying near each other. Ideally these ropes should be placed in position by the facilitator prior to viewing by the group, so that the true linked or unlinked nature of the ropes is not accidentally revealed. Two different colors of half-inch-diameter (12.7 mm) rope, approximately 13 to 20 feet (4–6 m) in length, can be used for this activity, or two different-colored Raccoon Circles, which are 15 feet (4.6 m) in length.

Next, invite your audience to view the ropes and ask participants to stand on the left side of the ropes if they believe these two ropes are linked and stand on the right side of the ropes if they believe they are unlinked. It is typical for some members of the group to be on each side of the ropes, although one side is likely to have a slight majority.

This is the perfect moment for introducing a tool to the group to assist them in their quest for consensus. We call this tool "pairing and sharing." Ask every person from one side to link elbows with a single partner from the opposite side and form a small, two-person committee. Each person now has the task of convincing his or her partner why the partner should join him or her on that side, or listening carefully to his or her partner and considering altering his or her choice to form consensus within this small group.

Even after a few minutes of discussion, it is likely that you'll still have participants on both sides maintaining their difference of opinions. Rather than quickly pulling on one of the ropes to discover if it is actually linked or unlinked, inform the group that you intend to pull one of the ropes slowly and that they are allowed to change sides at any time they choose. The fact is that when the facilitator pulls on one of the ropes, the members of the audience get more information that can help them to make a better decision. By using this technique, even participants who have made an incorrect choice are allowed to learn from their mistake and are welcomed to the other side.

While the actual solution may be simple or complex, the real value of this activity comes from a team working together to achieve a group consensus, listening to each other, and learning the skills that it takes to get everyone on the same page. The pairing and sharing process is very important and involves everyone working with a partner in an attempt to convince one other person before trying to convince the entire group. This technique is not only useful in problem-solving situations like the Missing Link but can also be used with other work-related problems and challenges.

After revealing the true nature of the tangled ropes (linked or unlinked), talk with the group about their problem-solving techniques using the discussion questions provided.

There is one additional and subtle teachable moment that occurs in the Missing Link activity that can be very valuable in transforming the culture of an organization: the ability to recover from making a wrong decision. The simple act of allowing participants to change their decision when more information becomes available enables the behavior suggested by John C. Maxwell in his appropriately titled book *Failing Forward* and is further substantiated in the book by Tim Harford, *Adapt: Why Success Always Starts with Failure.*

The ideal time to introduce your audience to this activity is just before they are required to make a collaborative decision about something. By teaching them helpful tools, such as the pairing and sharing process, they become more aware of other points of view and ultimately are able to make a choice based upon a higher quality of reasoning and information than one made only for their own point of view. This is a truly powerful and practical set of skills, to be sure.

The dilemma presented in this activity is likely to produce two camps of participants: those who believe the ropes are linked and those who do not. This situation is classically referred to as the storming stage in the theory of group development. For groups to move forward from this stage to a more productive stage, tools are needed to overcome their disagreement. For more information about the stages of group development, refer to the following articles by Bruce W. Tuckman, professor of education at Ohio State University:

- Tuckman, Bruce W. "Developmental Sequence in Small Groups." *Psychological Bulletin* 63, no. 6 (1965): 384–399. [The original article]
- Tuckman, Bruce W. "Developmental Sequence in Small Groups." *Group Facilitation: A Research and Applications Journal* 3, Spring (2001): 66–81. [A look back, 35 years after the original groundbreaking article]

For a wider presentation of the group development process, *Theories of Small Group Development* by Raye Kass presents five significant theories and contrasts their similarities and differences.

Discussion Questions

1. How many people changed sides because of their partner's beliefs?

2. For the side that was eventually correct, why didn't they manage to attract more people to their side?

3. How many people were sure the moment they first saw the ropes, which side was the right side?

4. How many people changed sides several times, and still weren't sure?

Word Circles

Group Size
Up to 25

Materials
Word cards and help cards

Time
20 minutes

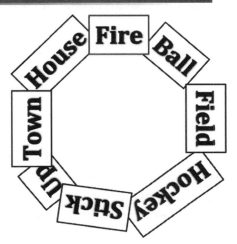

Procedure

Multiple Intelligence (MI) theory proposes that people learn best when taught or trained in a style compatible with their particular intelligence or strength. A variety of intelligences have been identified, and these include:

Visual-Spatial	Mastery of shapes, diagrams, colors, maps, and visual objects
Verbal-Linguistic	Mastery of words and language, written and spoken
Logical-Mathematical	Mastery of reasoning, problem solving based on logic/math
Bodily-Kinesthetic	Mastery of movement, dance, athletics, manipulation
Musical	Mastery of sound, rhythms, melodies, and lyrics
Natural-Environmental	Mastery of natural phenomena, processes, and patterns
Interpersonal	Mastery of empathy, connection with others
Intrapersonal	Mastery of internal feelings, thoughts, self-awareness

Add to these familiar multiple intelligences such additional themes as emotional intelligence, spirituality, existentialism, and humor, and you have a long list of potentially interesting and creative methods for training your staff. The Word Circle puzzles that follow are just one example of an intelligence-specific (in this case, verbal-linguistic) activity.

Word Circles are a new and unique way to linguistically challenge your team. You can use this type of activity as a problem-solving activity, an activity to promote communication, a mid-training energizer, and even a team-building activity.

Word Circles are a fun and interesting challenge for a facilitator to create and for a group to solve.

Begin by placing each of the following words on a separate index card: Bar, Bell, Bowl, Block, Building, Buster, Day, Dream, Game, Hole, Hop, Punch, Tape, Team, Scotch, Worm.

Then shuffle this collection of cards. This particular Word Circle puzzle contains 16 words. You can create your own Word Circle puzzles with as many words as you have participants.

In addition to the word cards, you'll want to also create three help cards to assist the group in completing the task. Each card includes one of the following phrases:

Ask one yes or no question.
Tell us one word combination.
Is this combination correct?

Now combine the word cards and the help cards into one deck and pass out one card to each member of your group, and the challenge begins. The goal is to correctly place each member of the group in the proper order so that each word forms an acceptable combination with the word before it and after it.

Some word combinations, although acceptable, do not allow a complete circle to be formed. Flexibility, adapting to change, problem solving, communication, teamwork, and tenacity are all needed here to complete the task. For the 16-word puzzle presented here, the correct Word Circle combination is: Team, Building, Block, Buster, Bar, Bell, Hop, Scotch, Tape, Worm, Hole, Punch, Bowl, Game, Day, Dream.

There are many similarities between this activity and any group of the same size working on a group project. As such, the debriefing or reviewing questions can help identify opportunities where the performance of the team here can be compared to the performance of this same team when working on a joint project in the workplace.

Variations

If you'd like to incorporate another intelligence into the Word Circle challenge, consider replacing each word card with a picture card of that same subject. In other words, replace a card with the word *Book* with a card showing a picture of a book. This technique will enable you to combine the verbal-linguistic (language) intelligence with the visual-spatial (picture) intelligence.

Tips

For specific training programs, try to incorporate key words or phrases from your training curriculum into your Word Circle puzzles. Begin by identifying the total number of cards you would ideally like to have in your Word Circle. Then begin with one of the words you'd ideally like to include. Next, check a dictionary for potential word combinations with this chosen word, and select one of these combinations to build the next link in your Word Circle puzzle. Continue adding words (without duplicating any previously used) until you have about three-quarters of the Word Circle formed. Next, try to select the remaining words so that you can build a bridge back to the original first word, in exactly the number of cards required—a challenging task for sure, but exciting when you find just the right combination. Don't forget, you only need to have approximately the number of Word Circle pairs as the number of participants, because some participants can be given the help cards.

Discussion Questions

1. What role did you play in this activity? Did you assume your position yourself, or were you instructed to locate there?
2. Did you attract others to you, or did you go to join them?
3. Were you able to help others find their location? Did you use the available resources (such as the help cards) to accomplish this task?
4. Was it difficult to encourage some people to move to other locations?
5. Was the solution process for this activity organized or chaotic?
6. What lessons did you learn from this activity that you can apply in the workplace?

13 Clues

Group Size
Any, split into teams of 6 to 8

Materials
One copy of the 13 Clues handout for each team, flip-chart paper, markers

Time
20 minutes

Procedure

Problems worthy of attack prove their worth by fighting back.
—*Piet Hein*

At the end of this activity description you'll find a challenging mystery presented via 13 clues. There is sufficient information here to solve the puzzle at hand. It is not easy but is certainly possible. This style of group challenge can be especially useful if you organize your audience into their personality or work style groups. Profile tools such as Myers-Briggs Type Indicator (MBTI), DiSC, True Colors, and other inventories traditionally separate a group into one of four or more different categories. Performing this activity with other group members of a similar work style can be illustrative as different problem-solving skills emerge and different solution strategies may be employed by each group. All groups typically solve this puzzle but often use different techniques. For this reason, it is helpful to supply each group with a single sheet of flip-chart paper and some colorful markers. At the conclusion of the activity, allow each group to present their solution and explain their problem-solving process.

Begin this activity by printing the clues provided here, cutting these clues into 13 different strips of paper, and placing them inside a standard unsealed postal envelope. After organizing multiple groups of six to eight people by their similar work styles, pass out the envelopes filled with clues and some "thinking paper" (such as flip-chart paper) and a few colorful markers. Encourage each group to record the details of their solution technique as they work to answer the question "In what order did the Swiss facilitators visit the various cities?"

The problem-solving techniques displayed by various work groups can vary significantly from each other, but many groups tend to use some form of a four-by-four matrix grid, similar to a Sudoku puzzle. Some groups will provide just the answer requested, while other groups will completely fill in every detail of who visited which location and when.

Upon completion of the task, invite each group to display their problem-solving process and share their analysis techniques. Look for opportunities to discuss problem-solving techniques that parallel the typical work-style behaviors of each group.

Discussion Questions

1. How would you describe your problem-solving process?
2. If you had to do this challenge again, what would you change about your process?
3. What strategies can you take back to the workplace?
4. How did the different teams or work styles approach this problem?
5. What method did another team or work style use that would have benefited your group?

Answer to 13 Clues

The answer to the question "In what order did the Swiss facilitators visit the cities?" is London, Montreal, Hong Kong, and Atlanta. The complete matrix of all cities and facilitators is shown below.

	Facilitators			
	Canadian	Swiss	English	Dutch
Cities Visited				
Montreal	1	2	3	4
Atlanta	2	4	1	3
London	3	1	4	2
Hong Kong	4	3	2	1

13 Clues

You may read this information out loud, but no one else may look at this paper.
Each group of facilitators visited the same four cities, but in a different order.

You may read this information out loud, but no one else may look at this paper.
The first place the Canadian facilitators visited was Montreal.

You may read this information out loud, but no one else may look at this paper.
London was the third city the Canadian facilitators visited.

You may read this information out loud, but no one else may look at this paper.
In what order did the Swiss facilitators visit the cities?

You may read this information out loud, but no one else may look at this paper.
The facilitators that bought reference books started their tour in Hong Kong.

You may read this information out loud, but no one else may look at this paper.
Some information is irrelevant and will not help solve the problem.

You may read this information out loud, but no one else may look at this paper.
The Swiss facilitators bought processing tools in London.
The English facilitators visited Hong Kong before Montreal.

You may read this information out loud, but no one else may look at this paper.
The Swiss facilitators visited Atlanta after Hong Kong.

You may read this information out loud, but no one else may look at this paper.
The Canadian facilitators bought cell phones in London.

You may read this information out loud, but no one else may look at this paper.
Each group visited their favorite city last.

You may read this information out loud, but no one else may look at this paper.
Four groups of facilitators from four different countries attended training events
in four different cities around the world.

You may read this information out loud, but no one else may look at this paper.
Of the four groups, the Dutch facilitators liked Montreal best.

You may read this information out loud, but no one else may look at this paper.
The Dutch facilitators bought reference books on their tour.

Blind Shapes

Group Size

6 to 14 (up to 11 participants playing the game with up to 2 observers and one facilitator)

Materials

Blindfolds for each participant, 25 small wooden objects (5 different shapes, with each shape in the same 5 different colors)

Time

30 to 45 minutes

Procedure

In our modern age of technology, the techniques available to us for communication are abundant and yet our ability to effectively communicate remains challenging. For many of us, face-to-face conversations have been replaced with telephone messages, voice mail, faxes, emails, and text messages, all of which have limitations that can distort the intended message. In order to be effective in our communications, it becomes necessary to transmit messages with clarity. The following activity will require just such clear communication.

The Blind Shapes activity begins with participants comfortably seated in a circle. A selected number of participants are blindfolded and the remaining sighted participants act in the role of observers. A single facilitator is present as well.

The collection of equipment for this activity consists of fabricated shapes that come in a variety of designs and colors. For the purpose of this activity, a complete set consists of 25 wooden pieces in five different shapes with each shape in the same five different colors, as shown in the illustration. Two random pieces are removed by the facilitator and the remaining

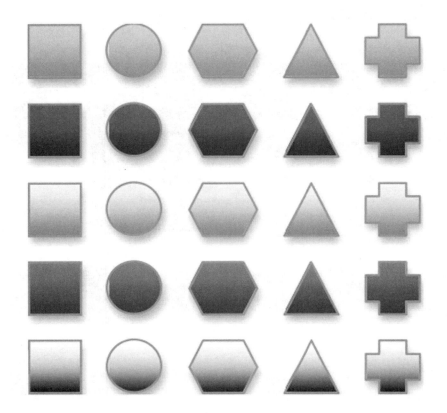

pieces are distributed to the blindfolded participants. Each blindfolded participant should ideally receive two or three random pieces.

The challenge for the group is to establish which two pieces are missing and what color they are. With blindfolds present, it is impossible for participants to determine color. For this information participants simply raise a single piece in their hand and ask their facilitator, "What color is this piece?"

The task is challenging, and groups occasionally have difficulty in the early stages of developing a process and working through their strategy, but all groups eventually complete the task. Strategies typically include first discussing one of the simplest (and easiest to describe) shapes and establishing a system that will work for other shapes as well.

The sighted participants in the group are invited to record their observations of the blindfolded group in the completion of their task. They should record such details as who provided leadership in the group and whether or not a breakthrough moment occurred.

At the completion of the activity, when the group has suggested which pieces they have determined are missing, blindfolds are removed and the observers are invited to share their insights, followed by insights from the entire group.

You can construct your own collection of shapes for this activity from your local craft store by purchasing wooden or plastic shapes (including three-dimensional objects) and painting them in bright colors. You can also purchase complete sets of the equipment for this activity, including blindfolds, from the sources listed here. The shapes provided in commercially produced sets are generally of a greater complexity than the standard geometric shapes shown in the previous illustration. The additional complexity and occasional similarity with other pieces further increase the clarity required when describing each shape.

Activity Name	Company	Location	Website
Colourblind	RSVP Design	UK	www.rsvpdesign.co.uk
CommuniCards	Metalog	Germany	www.metalog.de/
Blind Treasure	Akzente	Austria	www.trainings-shop.com
Blind Shapes	Training Wheels	United States	www.training-wheels.com

Discussion Questions

1. Other than being blindfolded, what was challenging about this activity?

2. Were all ideas heard? Why or why not?

3. Did you have a plan to accomplish your task?

4. Was a leader required? Did a leader emerge?

5. Did you eventually have a breakthrough? Can you describe the "breakthrough" moment?

6. Observers, what did you notice?

Handcuffs

Group Size

Any

Materials

One rope handcuff (described below) for each person

Time

10 minutes

Procedure

Here is a creative problem-solving activity that has been challenging audiences for more than 100 years. This active and engaging puzzle actually incorporates the members of your audience as part of the puzzle props, which adds a very human component to the challenge. But the best teachable moment in this particular challenge is that competition is diminished and group problem solving encouraged so that everyone in the group benefits from the suggestions and experiences of every other member of the group. If you are looking for an activity that requires close teamwork, here it is.

To begin this activity, invite the members of your audience to find a partner. Next, pass out one of the rope handcuffs to each person. These are 6-foot-long (2 m) segments of ordinary cloth utility rope (often used for clotheslines) with loops at each end.

Instruct one partner to place one hand in each of the loops on his or her rope handcuffs. The second partner places just one hand in a loop on his or her rope handcuffs and then passes the handcuffs over the partner's handcuffs before placing his or her second hand in the remaining loop. At this point both partners will have their hands in their own handcuffs and will be linked together.

The challenge to be solved is for each pair to become disconnected from each other without taking their hands from within the loops of their rope handcuffs and without untying the knots. But more importantly, inform your group that "we're all done, when we're *all* done." In this manner you'll move the Handcuffs challenge from being a competitive race for a solution to a true team problem-solving activity. The challenge is complete when everyone in the group is disconnected from his or her partner.

Initially, many groups attempt a kinesthetic solution by stepping over their partner's handcuffs and other various movements. When this technique does not produce a solution, encourage your audience to consider two things: what is working and what is not. Urge them to try new techniques. For example, you could try to increase the creative problem-solving ability in each group by joining four people together instead of just two. As the activity continues, you can further increase hints and clues to your audience by asking them to focus on the loops surrounding their wrists. The phrase "Look for a window of opportunity" can be helpful. In this case, the window of opportunity is the loop at the end of each rope handcuff. By passing one partner's rope through the loop and over the hand of his or her partner, it is possible to solve this puzzle.

If one or two pairs in the audience manage to find a solution to this puzzle, encourage them to assist others in completing the task as well.

Variations

One of the more interesting variations of this activity is to link eight to ten people together in a circle. The solution technique is exactly the same as for two people, but the group problem-solving process will be substantially different given the limited mobility this configuration allows.

Another version of Handcuffs that removes all kinesthetic components to the creative problem-solving process incorporates the use of a chain-link fence. Place one partner on each side of the fence, passing the rope handcuffs through to link them together. Now have the partners analyze how to disconnect from each other.

For indoor programs where a chain-link fence is not easily accessible, place a line on the floor between partners and inform them that they cannot cross the line during their problem-solving attempts.

A final variation invites both partners to remain seated while disconnecting from each other.

Teachable Moments

The concept of working through a problem that seems to have no obvious solution is a valuable work skill. Creativity and out-of-the-box thinking are required. Retracing the steps between the initial presentation of the puzzle and the ultimate solution provides a road map for future investigations and solutions to other problems, challenges, and puzzles. Finding the solution as part of a group effort and sharing this solution with every member of the group is also a lesson in abundance and creates an atmosphere of information sharing that can be extremely helpful to the members of a group.

But most of all, facilitators should try to go beyond solving only the basic puzzle. Learning how to disconnect two rope handcuffs is unlikely to be significant in the world of big business, but learning how to systematically solve a problem that initially appears to have no solution has endless applications in the real world. Now that your audience has solved this puzzle together, what other challenges are they facing where some of these same problem-solving techniques could be helpful?

You can find variations of this activity in publications dating back to the 1800s. One such publication shows partners joined together by string handcuffs passed through the keyhole of a closed door, which promoted us to try the version with partners standing on two sides of a chain-link fence.

Discussion Questions

1. What did it take to discover a solution?

2. How would you rate your attitude during the activity?

3. How did you overcome any frustration you may have felt?

4. What did you learn that you could apply to difficult challenges in the workplace?

16-Card Puzzle

Group Size
Any, split into teams of 4 to 7
Materials
One deck of cards for every three teams
Time
10 minutes

Procedure

> When I am working on a problem, I
> never think about beauty. I think only
> how to solve the problem. But when I have finished, if the solution is
> not beautiful, I know it is wrong.
> —*R. Buckminster Fuller*

Beyond the simplicity of this activity is the opportunity to actively explore the creative problem-solving process. In other words, finding a solution to this puzzling challenge is just the first level of the experience. Understanding how to go about the creative problem-solving process and extending this understanding to other current challenges and problems in the workplace are higher applications of knowledge.

For this card activity, you'll need 16 regular playing cards consisting of four different card values in four different suits. A regular deck of 52 playing cards has sufficient cards for three of these 16-card puzzles.

The challenge here is to place each of the 16 cards in a four-by-four matrix so that no two cards of the same suit or the same face value are in the same vertical column or horizontal row. One example of a solution is shown here. For this particular case, geometric symmetry was incorporated, starting with the placement of the four aces and the four kings. The remaining jacks and queens were also placed symmetrically, completing

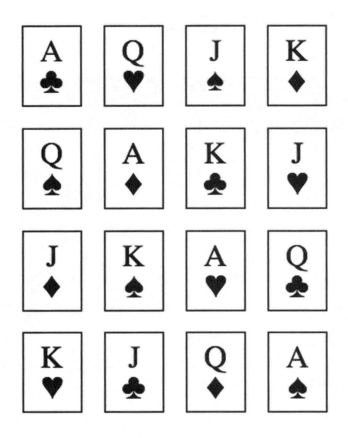

the puzzle. The use of symmetry then becomes one of the tools that can assist in the creative solution to such a problem. What other tools can be identified and applied to help in this situation?

A Second Playing Card Puzzle

This second playing card puzzle requires one complete suit from a regular playing card deck. From this collection of 13 cards, participants are asked to select any 12 cards and to place these cards in the configuration shown so that the sum of the face values on each four cards in any row or column add up to the same number. In this case, face cards have their own unique values, such as the jack, which has a face value of 11; the queen, which is worth 12; and the king, with a face value of 13.

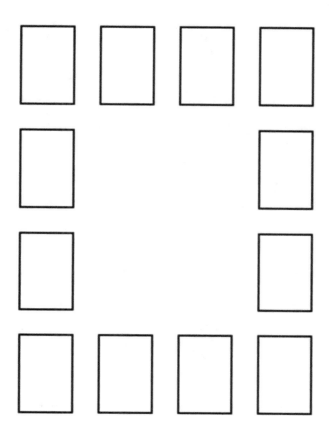

As stated here, this card puzzle has quite a few challenges. First, the dilemma of which 12 cards to select or conversely which card to eliminate is a critical decision. Or is it? Is it possible to complete this task no matter which card is eliminated?

Next, what is the value of the sum for each side? Without knowing this value, a straightforward, brute-force solution is unlikely. Instead, a more general solution must be found. Although frustrating, it is exactly this style of general problem-solving ability that is highly valued in the workplace. The ability to analyze a problem and identify which factors are critical to the solution is an admirable skill. The process by which various groups in your training audience solve this puzzle is worthy of discussion.

As a facilitator you have the option to introduce this puzzle in the generic form presented here, or you can choose to include a bit more information.

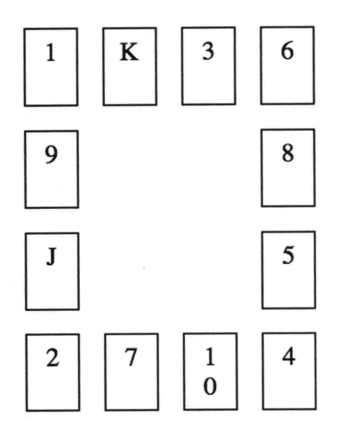

For example, if you remove the queen, the puzzle can be completed with the remaining cards, with each side of the square pattern adding up to 23, as shown here.

Discussion Questions

1. How did you solve this puzzle?
2. If you had to devise a "template" for solving problems of this nature, what would it look like?
3. How can you apply this process to other challenges and problems in the workplace?

Modern Hieroglyphics

Group Size

Any

Materials

One copy of the Modern Hieroglyphics handout for each participant, pencils

Time

10 minutes

Procedure

We hope you enjoy these word puzzles. There is one for every letter of the alphabet, and a few are sure to challenge you and your team's linguistic skills.

Pencils and copies of the puzzles included in the Modern Hieroglyphics handout are all that is needed. You can present these puzzles via an overhead projector and transparencies, computer-generated images, images or papers mounted on the walls, or flash cards made from index cards. You can find additional puzzles in many newspapers or create your own by using the words associated with your organization, corporation, or group.

Teachable Moments

There is often a moment of insight, sometimes referred to as a BFO (Blinding Flash of the Obvious), between gazing at one of the word puzzles that follows and the realization of what it is trying to tell you. Decoding ciphers, ancient languages, secret messages, encrypted documents, or, in this case, very modern versions of hieroglyphics with a few modern pictograms thrown in for good measure can be a fun way of stimulating the portion of the brain that deals with words, language, and speech. While the rules that define the word puzzles in this activity do not follow the standard rules of grammar, they do encourage participants to look carefully at each puzzle and interpret what the writer was hoping to convey. In a similar fashion, after decoding a few of these word puzzles, present your group with a paragraph from their own organization such as a mission statement, rules of conduct, a vision statement, core values, policy information, a letter of praise for a job well done, or some other written commentary. Next, have the group decode this document in a similar fashion to the word puzzles in this activity. By rewriting the document in their own words and creating clarity and discussion around the content, you will have raised their level of involvement with this information and greatly increased their retention of this material.

You can also use this activity to discuss perspective (looking at things in a different way). Sometimes the answers are right in front of us, we just need to adjust our vision or perspective, to see it.

The ability to decipher or to read people is a valuable skill for both team members and team leaders. The field of neuro-linguistic programming (NLP) focuses on this concept. For more information on this topic, read *NLP at Work: The Essence of Excellence* by Sue Knight.

Variations

Create word puzzles that include words and topics familiar to your organization, department, school, summer camp, or corporation. Consider incorporating international words, phrases, and themes for culturally diverse organizations.

Discussion Questions

1. What happened when you worked together to answer the questions?

2. Did everyone have the same perspective?

3. What were you able to learn from your teammates?

4. How does this apply to difficult tasks at work?

Modern Hieroglyphics

Below are words that say one thing, and mean another.
Decode each of the cryptic messages below and write the true message below each clue. For example, bit MORE decodes as "a little bit more."

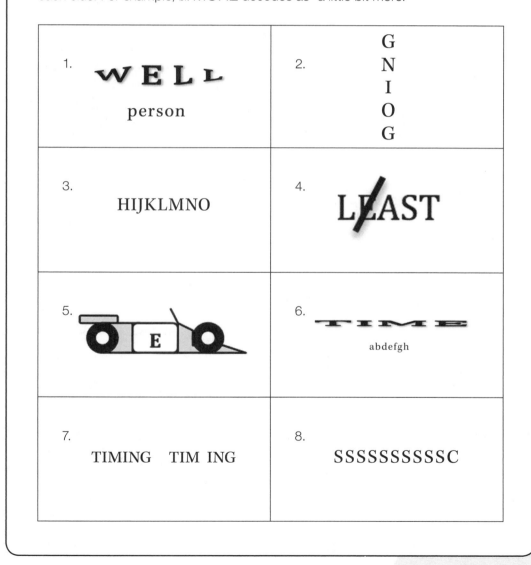

1. W E L L
person

2. G
N
I
O
G

3. HIJKLMNO

4. L/AST

5. E

6. TIME
abdefgh

7. TIMING   TIM ING

8. SSSSSSSSSSC

9. **Red** Lips Lips	10. S S T T A A R R E E
11. SOMETH	12. 2 UM + 2 UM
13. **M.D.** **Ph.D.**	14. ME NT
15. _____it	16. ISSUE ISSUE ISSUE ISSUE ISSUE ISSUE ISSUE ISSUE ISSUE ISSUE

Modern Hieroglyphics Answer Key

1. Well-rounded person

2. Going up

3. Water (H_2O)

4. Last but not least

5. Eraser

6. Long time no see

7. Split-second timing

8. Tennessee

9. Red tulips

10. Downstairs

11. The beginning of something big

12. Forum

13. Paradox

14. Apartment

15. Blanket

16. Tennis shoes

Arrowheads

Group Size

Any, split into teams of 4 to 7

Materials

One set of arrowheads for each team (created from the Arrowhead Template provided)

Time

10 minutes

Procedure

Here is a puzzle that creates a specific teachable moment related to completing a task with limited resources. With the desire to achieve higher return on investment (ROI) for all major projects, minimizing the resources required to complete a task is a common reality in the business world. This goal is even more present today, when earth-friendly and environmentally green policies encourage minimal use of our most precious resources. This puzzle will explore this topic by demonstrating that it is possible to complete a challenging assignment even when the resources provided seem insufficient.

Prior to this activity, make four photocopies of the Arrowhead Template found on the following page. Next, cut three of these arrowheads into two unique pieces, as shown in the cutout. This will give you one set of arrowheads. Make enough so each group has a set to work with.

The challenge is to use these seven pieces to create a total of five arrowheads. That's right, five arrowheads. Each arrowhead will be the same size and shape as the others, and all five arrowheads will be visible at the same time. There is one complete arrowhead within the puzzle. This will serve as a template for the other arrowheads, which will all be this same size and shape. Now considering that you used four arrowheads to create this puzzle, using these same arrowheads to create five arrowheads seems highly unlikely. But fear not, it is indeed possible. As shown in the illustration below, the seven pieces are used to construct the original four arrowheads, and these four arrowheads, when used properly, create the boundary of the fifth arrowhead in the center—an arrowhead that is exactly the same size and shape of the other four arrowheads.

The ability to complete a task even with limited resources is the teachable moment of this puzzle. In this particular case, efficient usage of the resources present enabled the formation of the fifth arrowhead. To transfer the solution of this puzzle back to your audience's work environment, begin by asking what current projects seem to 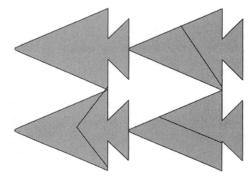 lack sufficient resources to be successfully completed. Next, inquire what techniques were used in the solution of the arrowhead puzzle that could be used in the workplace. Finally, create a link between the successful solution to the arrowhead puzzle and potential solutions to current challenges in the workplace.

As an additional teachable moment, consider the following scenario. The arrowhead puzzle presented here is an excellent example of synergy. The sum of the whole is greater than the sum of the parts. In this case, even with what seem to be insufficient resources, it is possible to create more with less.

Imagine that you have a workforce with ten employees in a particular department. Business is good. So good, in fact, that you choose to expand your business by a factor of 10. You have a good business sense and understand what the ten present members of your team can accomplish. It only seems to reason that a workforce of 100 should be able to produce ten times what your current workforce produces. But herein lies the mystery of many corporations. Ten times the workforce does not necessarily produce ten times the output.

In the neutral case, ten times the workforce, with similar resources and skills, should ideally be able to produce ten times the output. But sometimes those additional workers are forced to share the same resources or they have difficulties that become apparent with 100 employees but were hidden in a group of only ten. In this case, the output from the larger employee pool is actually less than ten times. The best-case scenario is when the workforce is multiplied by a factor of 10, and more than ten times the output is achieved. This is synergy in action. The combined effort of the larger workforce helps streamline the process, creates a larger pool for ideas and solutions, and builds an atmosphere of excellence.

From this simple example, you can see that teams operating synergistically have a substantial advantage over teams that do not.

You can create your own arrowhead puzzle using heavy paper, cardstock, cardboard or plywood by using the template shown at the end of this activity.

Discussion Questions

1. What projects are you working on now that appear to lack sufficient resources?
2. After successful completion of this challenge, might you reconsider your perspective?
3. What specific techniques did you use today that you could use in the workplace?

Arrowhead Template

A Quick Study

Group Size
   Any
Materials
   Poster board, whiteboard, or flip chart; markers
Time
   10 minutes

Procedure

Here is a convenient way to demonstrate the power of education and training. Begin by arranging each of the 26 letters of the alphabet as shown. It is best to do this on a large and easily visible poster board, whiteboard, or flip chart.

$$\text{A E F H I K L M N T V W X Y Z}$$
$$\text{C O S}$$
$$\text{B D G J P Q R U}$$

Next, ask for a volunteer from your audience and tell them that you can train them how to replicate this exact list of letters in less than a minute. Take this person a few steps away from the rest of the group and quickly explain that the criteria that divide these letters are straight letters (e.g., H), curved letters (e.g., C), and a combination of straight and curved (e.g., P). Then bring this person back to the group and ask him or her to draw the three categories correctly on a fresh sheet of paper. To the amazement of the rest of the group, this person will be able to exactly replicate this activity's seemingly complicated collection of letters, with no more than a minute's worth of training—thus providing a truly amazing display of the power of education.

You can take this opportunity a step further and display the following collection of letters, but this time only for ten seconds.

ABDOPQR
CEFGHIJKLMNSTUVWXYZ

Ask for a new volunteer and quickly explain that the criteria this time are letters with enclosed space (e.g., O), and those that do not have any enclosed space (e.g., T). Again, the participant will quickly be able to reproduce your list of letters with almost magical ability.

You can perform this amazing feat of education using letters written on a flip chart or whiteboard; letters projected onto a screen; letters individually written on index cards; or wooden, plastic, and even magnetic letters available in craft, toy, or hardware stores. You can also replace the letters of the alphabet with the numbers zero through nine, using the same criteria as presented here.

Teachable Moments

The speed at which volunteers can be educated to replicate what appears to be a complicated collection of letters is almost magical in nature. Use this activity to demonstrate to your group how educational techniques can help to minimize some of their fears related to learning new information or challenging procedures in training programs.

The educational process used in this activity is called "sense-making." It is the ability to identify the smallest details that make each ordering of letters meaningful. When teaching, training, and facilitating a group, you can present the content of your choice, but if you also show them where this information should be applied, you'll help them make sense of the content and be much more capable in the use of it in the future. Simply stated, sense-making makes sense!

Discussion Questions

1. What were your thoughts as your colleague was able to replicate the original order so quickly?

2. With your new skills, could you do it?

3. How can you use this technique?

Nail Puzzle

Group Size

Any, split into teams of 7

Materials

For each team: 2 blocks of wood, 22 16p nails

Time

10 minutes

Procedure

To those of us who use experiential activities, paradise looks a lot like a large hardware store with no cash registers. Consequently, we frequently use quite a few hardware store items in the creation of these team- and community-building activity props. The Nail Puzzle that follows is just one example of how hardware can create a significant teachable moment.

In the book *Vital Friends*, author and Gallup poll expert Tom Rath makes a compelling case for the value that positive relationships and friendships can have in the workplace. That the engagement of employees at work who have a best friend present is eight times greater than the engagement of those without friends in the workplace is a significant piece of data. That

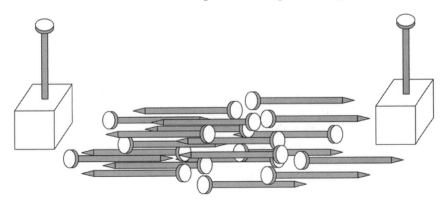

employees with three or more friends in their workplace consider the quality of their work life outstanding is yet another. Consider the following puzzle challenge to illustrate the value that positive relationships and connections have in the workplace.

"You are presented with two blocks of wood, into which large 16p nails have been placed. These nail tower blocks are then located precisely 7 inches (18 cm) apart on the surface of a table or desk. Twenty additional nails are available to build a bridge between the two nail towers so that this bridge only makes contact with the two vertical nails, but not the wood blocks or table surface. Ready, set, go!"

As a corporate metaphor, consider the two nail towers on page 175 as two divisions of one corporation (perhaps the sales and manufacturing divisions, for example). The bridge to be built between these groups is basically the working relationship between the members of each division. A good bridge equals a productive working relationship.

The challenge of building a bridge between these two groups, even with double the initial supply of nails, seems unlikely if not impossible. Yet it is exactly this kind of corporate situation that makes relationship building so difficult between entities of the same company.

After your group has pondered the above situation, and perhaps even attempted several potential solutions, show them the following solution.

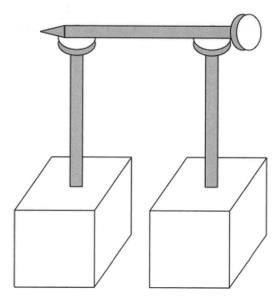

The solution to this problem (like so many other relationship problems in the corporate world) becomes so much easier (and more cost effective, and requires less resources, and takes less time) if the first thing you do is bring the two groups closer together!

"But you didn't say we could do that!" cry the members of your audience. "We thought the locations of those two nail towers were fixed!" After which you can turn to them, and in your most sincere and humble voice, say, "From this moment forward, for the rest of your working life, you have permission to do whatever you can to build strong relationships with the members of your team, your division, and your company. If that means moving some things around, or modifying the guidelines, or trying something that has never been tried before, you have permission to do so."

By simply moving the two nail towers closer together, the task of building a bridge between the two towers becomes simple. So simple, in fact, that a single nail can be used to accomplish the task. Why then is it so difficult, or to use a more demonstrative phrase, so against the present corporate culture to move the towers closer together? Some will say, "But you placed the towers a few inches apart for a reason!" Okay, but what is it about that reason that keeps you, the empowered team member, from changing it, especially if it means successfully completing the task?

This insight provided by this simple puzzle can be extremely helpful when making a case for building and enhancing positive relationships within a corporation. The existing corporate culture, in this case, provides the framework (two nail towers a set distance apart), the resources (20 nails and the members of the team), and the goal (building a bridge) for the team to accomplish. Is the team empowered enough to suggest solutions that require modifying the corporate culture, or are they constrained to working within the traditional framework to accomplish the task? What is the resistance of the team to moving the towers? What does moving the towers closer together represent in the actual workplace? How much time, energy, and resources were used trying to solve this problem while the towers were still inches apart?

If we are to successfully complete tasks like the one above, and reduce the time, energy, and resources used in the completion of our work, then we must first establish a corporate culture that fosters this result. We must "bring the group closer together" first. We must build a connection between the members of the group that lasts longer than a single day team-building program. We need more than an awareness level of interest on the part of the team members. We need real skills, real community, unity, and connection between members of the team, and we need a corporate strategy that embraces these characteristics today and in the future. We need to make stronger connections within our workforce, and keep those connections strong.

(Author Jim Cain created this nail puzzle as a means to demonstrate the necessity of bringing groups together in the corporate world.)

Discussion Questions

1. How would you rate the difficulty level of this task?

2. Were your biggest challenges real or assumed?

3. What kind of assumptions do we make in the workplace that may prevent us from building bridges with other people?

4. What can we do to build more meaningful connections at work?

Tangrams

Group Size

Any, split into teams of fewer than 10

Materials

One tangram puzzle for each team, 100-foot rope

Time

10 to 20 minutes

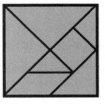

Procedure

Puzzle enthusiasts recognize tangrams as one of the oldest and simplest of puzzles, but still a worthy challenge. Here are a few interesting ways that you can incorporate tangrams actively into your program, encourage participation and group interaction, and create teachable moments as well.

Begin by either creating your own tangrams (using the Tangram Template at the end of this activity as a guide) or purchasing several tangram sets (typically available in toy stores, puzzle and game stores, or educational supply stores).

Simply placing the seven tangram shapes on a table will encourage participants to begin playing with these geometric shapes. Traditionally tangram pieces were assembled to create the outline of familiar objects. A silhouette or shadow image illustrating the outline but not the interior details is typically presented. Participants then try to place each of the seven shapes in the proper location to create this shape. See if you can create the following shapes using the seven traditional tangram pieces.

Beyond the simple challenge of the tangram are opportunities for team-work and learning. Here are a few activities that explore various training themes.

Underwater Scenario

In this shipwreck simulation, your team of divers has found a unique underwater treasure. Before bringing it onto the deck of your research vessel, divers must assemble the tangram into a perfect square (to make sure all the pieces are present). Since the puzzle was found in reasonably shallow water just 16 feet (5 m) deep, divers can access the discovery site without underwater breathing devices or communication equipment.

Each person in the group is allowed one "dive" or visit to the discovery site to attempt to create a square from the tangram pieces. The additional challenge of this activity is that participants can only stay "underwater" and work on the tangram puzzle for as long as they can hold their breath.

Begin with the entire team standing around the outside perimeter of a long rope, 100 feet (30 m) in length, which has been formed into a circle. In the center of the circle, place seven very large tangram pieces in random order (including upside down). The task for the group is to assemble these tangram pieces into a perfect square within the boundary of the rope circle. Team members enter the circle one person at a time and they must hold their breath for the duration of the time they are inside the circle. The circle is essentially an imaginary swimming pool and the tangram pieces are located "underwater." Since participants would not be able to hear underwater, communication can only occur on dry land (outside the perimeter of the circle). By requiring participants to hold their breath while inside the circle, facilitators encourage all group members to become involved in the solution process, not just a select few.

To further assist (or instruct) the group, you can add words, graphics, illustrations, or additional information to each tangram. As an example, you might add the seven most significant words from a corporate mission statement. Another option would be to create a corporate logo or illustration on the tangram pieces and then assemble them.

Walking Around Tangrams

This supersize version of tangrams is produced by creating a large-scale set of plywood tangrams and placing a foot strap in the middle of each piece. Seven participants can move around with a single piece attached to one of their feet and attempt to find the correct location for their contribution to the puzzle. You can also use this version for Speed Tangrams where multiple teams compete to complete their tangram shapes as quickly as possible.

Tangrams for Exploring Diversity and Uniqueness

Shown below is the traditional tangram puzzle followed by three other tangram-like variations. Make each of these shapes from a different color and you'll have the opportunity to discuss diversity issues as part of your puzzle solving.

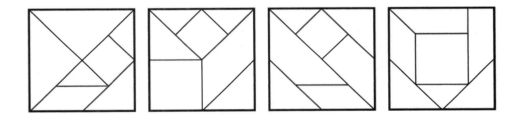

After providing each group of four to six participants with one of the above collections of geometric pieces, ask them to create various shapes, and see how many of these same shapes can also be made by each of the other groups, using their own unique pieces. You can ask your group some of the following questions:

- What shapes or patterns do we all have in common?
- What shapes or patterns can each group uniquely make?
- Is it important that all groups are the same?

Notice that each of the four patterns, though different, do have several pieces in common with each of the other patterns.

The Diversity Quilt Tangram

Using the four different tangram-like patterns previously illustrated, with each pattern made from a different-color material, demonstrate that it is possible to assemble a square four times the size of each individual tangram, simply by bringing the four puzzles together. The Diversity Quilt challenge, however, is to reconstruct this same four-times-larger square without any pieces of the same color touching each other. The finished result will look a bit like a patchwork quilt.

While the four-color map theorem guarantees that it is possible to color any map geography with only four colors, this same theorem does not guarantee that any geometric figures will go together to fill an enclosed space.

Tangram Communication

As a communication activity, you can provide one person or small group with a tangram pattern already assembled. Their task is to verbally communicate to other participants or groups how to re-create this same pattern using their own tangram pieces. Initially, try this version with one-directional information only (that is, with only the presenter talking). Next, try another pattern but this time allowing feedback and two-way communication between the presenter and tangram builders.

Variations

You can make tangrams from a variety of materials (wood, plastic, paper, foamboard, cardboard, magnets, cloth, leather, stained glass, and yes, even food (if you choose to cut your square dessert cakes or gelatin desserts just right). With the right forethought, you can assemble tangrams on the ground, on tables, on walls (using spray adhesive or tape), on the ceiling, on a refrigerator (using magnets), on overhead transparencies (for projecting to a large audience), or anywhere else you can find the right combination of tangrams and space.

There are a variety of methods for dissecting a square into seven geometrical shapes. Four examples were shown previously. You can also create your own unique tangram-like shapes by dissecting the first square as follows. We recommend that you create straight lines following each of the grid lines, for simplicity in cutting and building other shapes. Two examples from this grid system are also shown.

One of the most helpful techniques to assist a team solving a tangram puzzle is to offer to place one or two pieces in the correct position, at the team's request. You can also provide an outline or framework to further identify the space the tangram puzzle will fill.

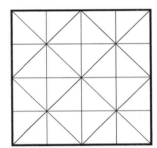 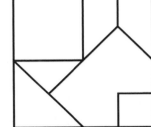 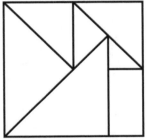

Dissecting the square   Two examples of seven-piece puzzles

Tangram Template

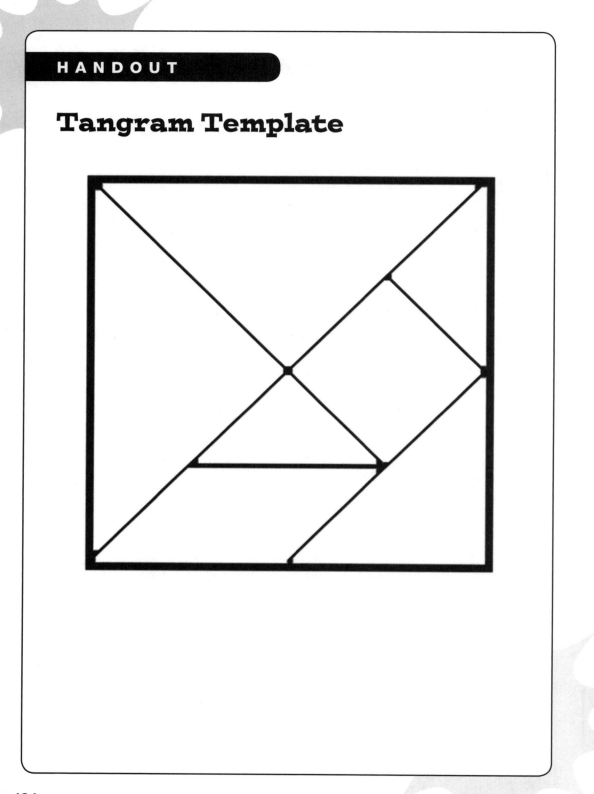

PVC Construction Project

Group Size

Any, split into teams of 4 to 7

Materials

A collection of PVC sections and connectors (one set for each team), International Space Station II handouts, pens or pencils

Time

30 to 40 minutes

Procedure

Construction projects that involve all the members of a group are ideal training activities that incorporate many of the same skills required for projects in the workplace. There are a variety of simple construction components that can be used, including toy construction sets, wooden blocks, or in this case PVC tubing and connectors. Plastic tubes and connectors are ideal construction props. They are lightweight, tactile, and easy to find or replace if needed, and they can be used to build a wide variety of familiar objects.

A group construction project is an excellent choice if you know the personality or work-style category of each of the members of your audience. Previously in this chapter, an activity entitled 13 Clues was presented that encouraged the formation of groups with similar work styles. The PVC Construction Project activity presented here encourages the formation of groups where a diversity of work styles is present, rather than having all the members in a group with identical work styles. This style of group formation is more realistic of the diversity in many work environments, and will allow group members to experience a wider diversity of group behaviors, problem-solving styles, processes, and actions.

Begin this activity in small groups of four to seven people. Each group is supplied with a collection of building materials, such as the PVC Teamplay Tubes shown in the photo on page 187. Next, inform each group of the challenge at hand. A few examples include:

- Construct the longest bridge possible, with no more than three PVC components touching the floor.
- Construct the tallest freestanding "basketball player statue" possible.
- Choose any 15 pieces and construct the tallest and most stable "tree" possible.
- Using all the pieces available, construct a "closed network" of tubes and connectors so that no openings are present. This particular construction project is often referred to as the International Space Station II Project.
- Using the least number of pieces possible, construct a freestanding coat (or hat) rack that can hold all the coats (or hats) from your group without touching the floor.
- Construct the tallest tower possible for a new cell-phone network in Chicago (the Windy City), then turn on a large fan and see what structures can withstand the forces generated by the wind.

While it is possible for a single facilitator to communicate the structure to be completed by the group, another possibility would be to supply each group with printed instructions and perhaps a few hints. This technique requires some interpretation by the members of each group and encourages more autonomy. Best of all, when the group has completed the task, the reverse side of the instruction sheet can contain questions for self-evaluating their own performance. A handout for this technique, which we call the International Space Station II, is provided here. This particular challenge requires that the number of PVC tubes must be twice the number of holes in all the various connectors present.

The goal is for each group to successfully complete their structure and then analyze the performance of their team by themselves at the completion of the project. While the challenge of successfully completing this task

is sufficient enough, the real opportunity in this activity is to provide a high-performing team with a project that they can accomplish by themselves, including a self-review of their performance at the completion of the project. By definition, this is exactly what a high-performing self-directed work team can do.

The International Space Station II

Project Description

Your team has been selected to create a prototype model of the next-generation space station for orbit around the moon. Using all of the PVC tubes and connectors available, construct one interconnected structure with no holes left open. Each PVC tube will have a connector at each end. Each PVC connector will have a tube in each opening. Here are a few hints that can assist you in your task:

- Use the connectors with the most holes first. Four-hole (crosses) and three-hole (Ts) connectors should be used before two-hole elbows and unions, leaving the one-hole cap for last.
- Use a variety of tube lengths throughout the building process. Do not use only long or short tubes in the beginning, but rather a combination of both lengths.
- It is possible to construct this model without reverting to forcing the PVC tubes and connectors together. If force seems required, consider rebuilding that portion of the model to reduce this level of stress.
- When you have completed the task, ask a member of your group to read the self-evaluation questions on the back of this page and discuss these as a group.

The International Space Station II

Self-Evaluation Questions

1. What role did each member of your team perform? Who was the leader? The organizer? The project coordinator? The creative genius? The problem solver? The cheerleader? What other roles were apparent during the completion of this task?

2. How much time was spent planning the project before actual construction began? In the future, would you recommend more or less of this planning time?

3. Which of the following styles of problem solving were used by your group? Circle one:
   a. Trial and error
   b. Analyze, plan, perform
   c. A really good guess and a whole lot of luck

4. After your group decided on a plan, did the group change the plan during the activity? If so, why?

5. How many ideas were considered during the early stages of the activity? Was each idea and each person given an opportunity to be heard?

6. Describe how each member of the group was given an opportunity to contribute to the group's success?

7. How would you rate your group's overall completion of this task?

8. In general, were the participants in your group more concerned about completing the task or about caring for the members of the group? On the "football field of leadership" below, mark the location where your team was focused.

   Completing the Care for the Members of the Group End Zone
   Task End Zone   10 20 30 40 50 40 30 20 10

9. If you had the opportunity to perform this task again, what would you do differently?

10. If you were asked to give advice to a new team trying to accomplish this assignment, what information would you provide to help them be successful?

11. If you were going to hire an employee to complete this task, what skills would you want that person to possess?

12. If you were chosen to lead the next group in successfully completing this activity, what style of leadership would you employ?

13. Some of the best things we learned during this activity were:

"I'm In" Games

Group Size
Any
Materials
Various props
Time
10 to 20 minutes

Procedure

"A few years ago I found myself in Paris. During the late afternoon, I paid a visit to a sidewalk café and for several minutes tried to get the attention of a waiter so that I could place my order. Now, Paris is a long way away for an Ohio farm boy and, as you can imagine, my grasp of the local language and customs was limited. Suffice to say that I was less than successful in my attempts, even as other customers around me were placing their orders, eating their food, and leaving. During this time, I noticed a new customer approaching and watched carefully how she placed her order. When she was finished ordering, I performed the exact ritual that I had seen her perform, and voilà!, I had discovered the secret."
    —*Jim Cain*

The following games are called by a variety of names, including "I'm in" and "never can tell" games. The challenge in each one is to carefully observe the facilitator and attempt to mimic his or her behavior in such a way that the facilitator will know you are "in" without giving away the secret to other members of the group. Careful observation and attention to detail are required to identify the subtle gestures, movements, or vocabulary required to join the ranks of those who are "in" on the secret.

You can use these games during breaks in the training process, or to produce teachable moments around careful observation, cultural awareness, language, gestures, and other common but sometimes misinterpreted mannerisms. It is important not to use these activities to exclude members of your audience but rather as a challenge to their observational skills. Be willing to repeat your clues multiple times, occasionally emphasizing the most critical information.

Polar Bears and Ice Holes (for the 21st Century)

You can have an ice hole without a polar bear, but you cannot have a polar bear without an ice hole.

The challenge in this activity is to discover what constitutes an ice hole, and what represents a polar bear, using whatever props the facilitator chooses to use. Typical props include dice, poker chips, jacks, or other small similar objects. Throw in a few additional random objects and you'll increase the level of challenge. Playing cards, pens, and paper clips are suitable.

In each round, the facilitator throws the collection of objects on the floor (or a tabletop), repeats the phrase above, and then asks, "So, how many ice holes and how many polar bears?" After a few guesses from the audience, the facilitator always gives the appropriate and correct number of each, then scoops up the objects and throws them again.

The solution of this "I'm In" Game is that only the dice are important here. All the other props are superfluous. An ice hole is the center dot (or pip) on the die face that displays one, three, or five dots. The polar bears are the dots surrounding these central dots, which are found only on the three and five faces of the dice. You can have an ice hole without a polar bear (the face showing one dot), but you cannot have a polar bear without an ice hole. The faces showing two, four, and six, for example, have no central dot. No ice hole, hence no polar bears.

The challenge for your audience is to sort through all the possibilities for what constitutes an ice hole or polar bear. Is it the number of dots on a playing card? Is it the total number of objects thrown? Is it only the red items? Is it a mathematical equation based upon some of the objects, but not all of them?

Eventually some members of the audience may stumble upon the correct representation of an ice hole and a polar bear. As you continue to play, discreetly remove one or more of the random objects not needed in each round, until eventually only the dice remain. In other words, keep repeating the game until only the most important objects (the dice) remain. After all, the goal is not to tell the audience the secret, but to repeat the presentation of the activity until each member of your audience can find the secret for him- or herself.

A Trip Around the World

The challenge of this game is to figure out what cities or countries should be next in line on your world tour. We begin the game with someone saying, "I'm going on a trip around the world, and I'm going to start in Amsterdam." The next person then says where he or she wishes to go next. In this example, the second person correctly says, "Toronto." The next person offers up his or her choice of city or country, and the game continues.

The mystery or secret of this activity is that the names of the cities or countries must begin with the letters in the phrase "a trip around the world" (or A – T – R – I – P – A – R – O – U – N – D – T – H – E – W – O – R – L – D), which could correspond to **A**msterdam, **T**oronto, **R**ome, **I**stanbul, **P**aris, **A**rgentina, **R**ussia, **O**maha, and so forth.

My Grandfather's Music Box

This is possibly the most difficult of the "never can tell" activities in this book, but it's a favorite for any group with musical talent (you'll understand why very soon).

> "My grandfather gave me a music box. It is a beautiful music box, but sometimes it doesn't play very well. However, if you put the right things into the music box, it plays beautiful music. For example, I could pour milk into the music box, and it plays just right. Or, I could put a sofa into the music box, and it would play twice as nicely. Oddly enough, however, if I put a couch into the music box, it doesn't play a single note. What would you like to try placing into the music box?"

These are things that make the music box play: *Doorknob, my father, mi casa, tigers.*

These are things that do not make the music box play: *Hinges, my mother, su casa, lions.*

As a hint to this mystery, think about the name of the song that the children in the movie *The Sound of Music* sing while they are frolicking through the countryside in clothing made from curtains. The objects placed into the music box "work" if they contain the two letters of any of the musical words *do, re, mi, fa, so, la,* or *ti.* So a couch will not work, but a sofa does (twice in fact, since it contains both *so* and *fa*). A <u>do</u>orknob works, as does a <u>ti</u>ger. And while tea is technically not identical to the musical word *ti,* it is phonetically close enough to pass muster in this activity.

Silly Tilly Williams

Silly Tilly Williams likes apples but not oranges. She likes doors but not windows. She doesn't like the sun, but she loves the moon. She likes kittens but not cats.

The goal of this verbal riddle is to find out the secret of what Silly Tilly Williams likes and dislikes. Begin by introducing Tilly, saying, "Silly Tilly Williams is a bit odd but not unusual. She likes doors but not windows. She doesn't like the ceiling but likes the floor. She likes football but not rugby. She likes skiing but not ice skating. She reads books but not magazines. She likes parallelograms but not circles."

When a member of the audience thinks he or she has Tilly figured out, that person tells the other members of the team something that Tilly likes and also does not like, such as "Silly Tilly Williams likes apples but not pears."

The secret of this activity (which is sometimes referred to as Green Glass Doors) is given away by Tilly's name. Silly Tilly Williams likes things with double letters. So she likes trees but not leaves.

Crossed or Uncrossed

This activity works best with participants seated in a circle of chairs (you'll find out why in just a few moments). You'll also need a pair of ordinary scissors with rounded or blunt tips.

Each person in the group repeats two critical messages as an ordinary pair of scissors is passed from person to person around the circle.

Those members of the audience who are "in" can instruct those just learning as they attempt to correctly state the nature of the scissors as either crossed or uncrossed. The first message is to state, "I receive the scissors _____," where the blank is filled in by the word *crossed* or *uncrossed*. The second message is, "And I pass them the scissors _____," where the second blank is also filled with the word *crossed* or *uncrossed*.

The secret to this game has nothing to do with the orientation or positioning of the scissors, but rather the legs of the people exchanging the scissors. If the person you receive the scissors from happens to have his or her legs crossed, then you receive them crossed. If, as you pass the scissors along to the next person in line, you happen to have your legs uncrossed, then you pass them uncrossed.

To add some additional mystery to this activity, participants can exaggerate opening or closing the scissors, turn the scissors over, pass the scissors with their right or left hands, change their seated posture, or use any other creative or distracting technique in an attempt to hide the true nature of what constitutes "crossed" or "uncrossed" in this activity.

Now that you know the secret, you can understand why sitting in chairs is appropriate. If you try this activity with everyone seated on the floor, chances are most people will have their legs crossed. When seated in chairs, there will be a variety of sitting styles, with legs both crossed and uncrossed. Be especially observant of participants sitting with their feet tucked under their chair, as it may not be immediately apparent whether they have their feet crossed or uncrossed at the ankles.

The Moon Is Round

A leader stands before the group and says the following phrase (while drawing the shape with his or her left hand):

"The moon is round *(draw a circle around your face)*, it has two eyes *(point your index and middle fingers toward your eyes)*, a nose *(point your index finger toward the tip of your nose)*, and a mouth *(draw a simple smile curve over your mouth with your index finger)*."

Audience members are then invited to replicate these same motions and words. Most will inevitably try to perform this task using the mirror-image hand (their right hand). The secret of the Moon Is Round is that you must replicate the movements with your left hand, not your right.

Magic Writing

Here is a very interesting way to send a coded message to your audience. This particular "I'm In" Game works best with your audience gathered around a table. You'll need a single pen (ideally one that doesn't have any ink) and a piece of paper. You won't actually need to write anything on the paper, but rather communicate through what you say and the manner in which you tap the pen on the table. See how many people can decipher this unique communication:

"Listen carefully." *Tap-tap-tap-tap.* "Very important." *Tap-tap.*

The correct answer is L-O-V-E. Let's try another one.

"Live in the moment." *Tap-tap-tap.* "Sometimes it isn't so easy."

"Too much information doesn't help." *Tap-tap.* "Nice try."

Here the answer is L-I-S-T-E-N.

While the creative and even theatrical movements of the leader are not important to solving this "I'm In" Game, they do provide a certain amount of misinformation that makes this particular activity even more challenging. A pen with no ink is ideal because members of the audience interpret the pen tapping as an attempt by the leader to try to get the ink within the pen to flow rather than as a code for the vowels within the secret word. This misdirection continues when participants that are "in" pick up the card at the completion of the word and clearly "read" what they see there.

The secret is to listen to the first letter in each phrase spoken by the leader. "Listen carefully," for example, communicates the letter *L*. "Nice try" communicates the letter *N*.

The pen tapping used in between phrases designates the correct vowel. One tap denotes the letter *A*, two taps for *E*, three taps for *I*, four taps for *O*, and five taps for the letter *U*.

The combination of coded phrases and pen tapping ultimately spells out the answer.

I Like Coffee, but I Don't Like Tea

If you listen carefully, the title of this game provides a hint about the secret. For example, "I like apples and oranges, but I don't like watermelon." "I like cars but not trucks, and I definitely do not like motorcycles, but bicycles are okay."

Like Silly Tilly Williams earlier in this section, I Like Coffee, but I Don't Like Tea is centered on the letters in each clue. In this case, I dislike things with the letter T and I like things that don't have that letter. So coffee is fine, but I don't like tea!

Discussion Questions

1. What is the advantage of games such as these?

2. What skills were required to figure out the puzzles?

3. How would these skills benefit us in the workplace?

6

Reviewing and Debriefing Techniques

Education's purpose is to replace an empty mind with an open one.

—Malcolm Forbes

Pairing and Sharing

Group Size
Any, paired up with partners

Materials
None

Time
5 minutes

Procedure

In an earlier section of this book, the opening activity The Big Question was presented as an activity that allows for a small-group (partner) experience even when a large number of participants are present. Pairing and Sharing uses this same technique during the reviewing process or at the closing end of the program. By minimizing the size of each reviewing group to partners, a facilitator can maximize the total number of participants actively speaking and provide a nonthreatening environment in which to share.

Begin this activity by asking everyone in your audience to find a partner who they shared a significant moment with during the day. Next, invite them to reflect upon the events of the day and share their personal insights, thoughts, feelings, goals, and experiences.

The value in this reviewing technique is that a proportionally greater group of individuals will be actively talking than if a single large group were present. The downside is that if something significant is shared between partners, other participants may not have the opportunity to benefit from hearing this comment. To minimize this disadvantage, you can provide an opportunity for a larger group interaction by inviting each of the small partner groups to share their most significant reflections with each other.

Variations

To make this activity a bit more kinesthetic, suggest that partners take a stroll together during their discussion. For an artistic component, provide each group with clay, crayons, markers, or other art supplies and ask them to create something that represents their experience.

The Magic Pot

Group Size
Up to 20

Materials
None

Time
10 minutes

Procedure

Here is a simple, no-prop, magical reviewing technique that encourages the processing of the experience by each participant. The Magic Pot also promotes self-assessment of team members' individual skills or talents that may be valuable to the group.

The Magic Pot used for this activity is an imaginary creation, similar to the one found filled with gold at the end of the rainbow. And since this container is magic, it is possible for participants to pull items of great value from the pot. The Magic Pot also has the capacity to hold enormous quantities of things that participants may wish to place in the pot.

Begin by inviting your audience to sit in a circle. Next introduce the Magic Pot debriefing technique:

> "I'd like you to imagine that I have in my hands a Magic Pot, similar to the kind you would find filled with gold at the end of a rainbow. We'll be using this particular Magic Pot today in two ways. First, you can reach into the pot and pull out something of great value that you experienced today. You might say, for example, that you learned

a great insight related to effectively communicating with your entire team today. Second, we don't want the pot to ever become empty, so in addition to taking things out of the pot, you can also place things back into the pot. You may have noticed, for example, that today you seemed to have quite a bit of positive energy, so you can place this into the Magic Pot. You are welcome to pull something out of the pot, place something into the pot, ask the other members of the group for assistance, or simply pass the Magic Pot along to the next person."

After introducing the Magic Pot to the group, the facilitator may want to demonstrate this technique by going first and then passing the Magic Pot along to another person in the group.

It can be helpful to ask everyone in your audience to think of what they would take or add to the Magic Pot prior to passing it around the group. This will enable participants to listen to others in the group as they present their findings, without using that same time to think about what they will say when their turn arrives. Even if a participant does not publicly share his or her thoughts during this activity, that individual still has had private time to internally process the day's experiences, which is also valuable.

Variations—An Improvised Magic Pot

Facilitators are a creative bunch! For the C5 Youth Foundation (www .c5leaders.org), experiential activities are a significant part of both their staff trainings and their youth development program. After a long weekend of staff training, the directors of the Boston-based affiliate wanted to hold one last debriefing session at camp just after the final meal and prior to driving back to their main headquarters a few hours away. By this time, all of the standard training equipment and supplies had been packed away, leaving few if any props available. One facilitator took this opportunity as a challenge and created an interesting reviewing technique in just a few minutes.

Looking around the room, she found three random objects and placed them inside an empty cardboard box. An old sports trophy, a plastic football, and a statistics textbook became useful metaphors for three specific themes: something you are proud of, something you can do very well, and any random thought you want to share. As the box was passed around the circle, participants reached in and carefully considered each object, and then presented their thoughts to the group. This is an excellent example of how even the most trivial or random object can become an effective reviewing tool, when thoughtfully presented to a group.

The Fishbowl

OBJECTIVE
- To practice focused listening

Group Size
Up to 20
Materials
30-foot rope
Time
10 minutes

Procedure

In this reviewing technique, participants can choose one of two different roles that they wish to play. There are *observers* who gather outside the perimeter of a large rope circle and *participants* who gather inside the rope perimeter. Participants are asked to consider the questions posed by the facilitator and each other and respond as appropriate. Observers have what some consider a more challenging role: to listen carefully to the participants but not respond until the very end of the discussion.

This activity begins with the facilitator preparing a rope circle sufficient in size to hold about half the audience present. Next, the facilitator chooses the topic of discussion and invites those who would like to participate or observe to move to the location of their choice.

What follows next is a discussion by only the internal members of the circle, which the external observers simply watch without adding their own commentary. At the very end of discussion by the participants in this activity, the facilitator has the choice of inviting commentary from the observers, or alternatively asking the group if they are ready to move on.

This reviewing technique can be powerful, especially in situations where conversation tends to go on indefinitely. The observer role is also enhanced when individuals are more focused on really listening to the members of the internal group than interpreting their discussion and preparing their own remarks. Throughout the day, make sure each member of your audience has the opportunity to be a member of both the observer and participant groups.

If you prefer a reviewing technique that allows participants to continuously and dynamically choose their role, consider using Step into the Circle, found on page 211.

Four-Minute Team

Group Size
Any
Materials
None
Time
4 minutes

Procedure

The closing activity in a training program can create significant memories for participants. Here is a very simple, no-prop activity that will leave a lasting impression with any group on the power of working together as a team.

Begin with your audience standing in random order within the available space (i.e., *not* standing in a circle). Next, share the following information with them.

"One of the ultimate tests of teamwork is for a team to collectively hold their outstretched arms in the air for four minutes."

Visually demonstrate this position for your audience with your arms outstretched, approximately parallel to the floor.

"It is almost impossible for an entire group to do this without teamwork. Let's see how well your team can perform in this final task. Ready, begin!"

It can be extremely uncomfortable to hold your outstretched arms in the air for four minutes. By placing your arms on the shoulders of other

team members, however, the challenge becomes easier for everyone! Typically, between minute one and two, some members of the group find this solution to ease their discomfort. Other members of the team quickly join them as they see the value of working together. This is a neat trick, a great metaphor for teamwork, and a memorable closing activity.

Discussion Questions

1. How did you facilitate this challenge?

2. How can you apply this to the workplace?

3. What did you learn?

Step into the Circle

Group Size
Up to 20

Materials
30-foot rope

Time
5 to 20 minutes

Procedure

Identifying which members of your audience are interested in actively participating (and speaking) during your program-reviewing process can be helpful, especially in large groups.

To begin this reviewing activity, invite the members of your audience to stand around the perimeter of a rope circle that has been placed on the floor. Next, pose a question to the group and invite anyone wishing to discuss this issue to move inside the circle. After sharing their opinions and

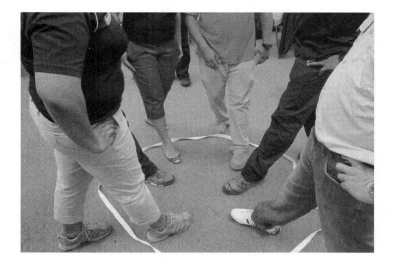

comments, participants are asked to exit and join the rest of their group around the perimeter of the circle. When the circle is empty, the facilitator can present another question or move on to the next activity.

This simple technique provides two significant opportunities in the reviewing process. First, anyone may choose to join the discussion by entering the circle at any time. Second, it is visibly apparent when the discussion is concluded (when the circle is empty) and the group is ready to move on.

Body Part Debrief

- To provide a metaphorical debriefing technique

Group Size
Any
Materials
Various props
Time
5 to 15 minutes

Procedure

This "Gray's Anatomy" of reviewing techniques is an effective way to generate discussion after your game or activity.

While there are dozens of practical objects that make for effective metaphorical reviewing subjects, this particular technique uses a very appropriate collection of body parts to express a surprising array of thoughts, ideas, and attitudes.

You can perform this reviewing activity in many different ways. Here are just a few suggestions:

- For a humorous version of the Body Part Debrief, find the Milton Bradley game Operation. This game identifies a variety of humorous body parts (such as the funny bone, Adam's apple, and charley horse). Next, ask the members of your audience who contributed to each of these essential body parts during today's training program.
- You can create a second version of this activity by downloading clip art or photographs from the Internet featuring your choice of body parts that illustrate key principles such as offering a helping hand (hand), showing backbone (spinal cord), speaking from the heart (heart), listening carefully (ear), seeing new things (eye). Place these images on index cards or laminated paper.
- A third version can be created by drawing a chalk outline of a complete body and asking your audience to identify some of the various body parts that were helpful in today's program. The brain, hands, and heart are typically suggested, but so are some of the more unusual and rare components, such as laughter, humor, and smiles (mouth); effective listening skills (ears); core values; and other character attributes.
- Our final version of the Body Part Debrief is a more tactile version and incorporates actual plastic or foam body parts, available from promotional printers and merchandisers that sell such unique objects, training prop suppliers (such as www.training-wheels.com), novelty stores, or toy stores that carry Mr. Potato Head (www.hasbro.com). You'll need a variety of parts, including ears (listening or something you heard today), eyeballs (something you saw today), hands (someone who gave you a helping hand or a push in the right direction or applauded your efforts), chattering teeth (conversation or perhaps biting off more than you could chew), foot (something that moved you), skull (that's using your head), spinal column (backbone, strength), and any other appropriate metaphorical body part. In this version, invite your audience to sit in a circle, and begin by identifying what each body part could represent, and then begin passing these around the circle. When someone receives a body part for which he or she identifies a connection, ask him or her to share it

with the rest of the group. A second technique for using actual foam or plastic body parts would be to ask each person to choose one prop and present it to another person in the group, providing some feedback as to why he or she deserves this particular part. "I'd like to give this funny bone to Steve today, for reminding us that laughter is very therapeutic to this group!"

Playing Card Debrief

OBJECTIVE
- To provide a fun way to debrief the training or activity

Group Size
Any

Materials
Playing cards

Time
10 minutes

Procedure

Here are several reviewing techniques that can be conducted with playing cards.

Playing Card Debrief for Large Groups

You'll need sufficient cards for each member of the audience. Begin by shuffling the deck and randomly passing out cards to each person. Next, inform participants the themes represented by each of the four card suits.

- Diamonds are a precious stone of high quality and value. Cards showing this suit encourage these members of your audience to reflect on high-quality or valuable things they have learned or experienced in this program.
- Clubs are associated with clover and other things that grow. This suit can represent the theme of growth or learning, the seeds of change, or something that was planted today and will grow in the future.
- Hearts designate something that comes from the heart or something that gives life to the process. Participants holding these cards are encouraged to speak from the heart about their experiences today.
- Spades bring in the theme of gardening and reflect something that was dug up today, something that has been cultivated, or perhaps something that was uncovered or discovered.

If you choose to include the two jokers in each deck of cards, these wild cards can be metaphors for a variety of additional reflection themes, including humor, surprises, unexpected experiences, or a wild card that is good for any theme.

After passing out the cards and allowing adequate time for personal reflection, invite small groups to form and members of these groups to share their insights relative to these themes.

Playing Card Debrief for Small Groups

Rather than passing out all the cards from a deck to your audience, limit the cards in this reviewing technique to the lower-value cards (aces, twos, threes, fours, and fives). Shuffle and pass out these cards to your group and, using the same suit themes as above, ask each person to share with a single partner the same number of comments about his or her theme as the value of their card (one through five). When the partners are finished, they can trade cards, reflect on their new theme, and move on to share with a new partner.

This technique encourages each person to reflect on several themes, deepening the reviewing process.

The Five Fs

Begin this reviewing technique by placing the five cards in a location easily seen by the members of your audience. Frame this activity by explaining that the five cards represent the five Fs, or specifically facts, findings, feelings, the future, and freedom.

- Facts are represented by the ace of diamonds. Discussion on this topic can include factual information from the program.
- Findings, represented by the ace of spades, include things that were discovered as a result of experiences from everyone in the group.
- Feelings, represented by the ace of hearts, include personal insights and emotions experienced.
- The future, represented by the ace of clubs, encourages participants to reflect on what will happen in the future as a result of today's program.
- The final card, the wild card or joker, reflects freedom on the part of the speaker and allows that individual to discuss any aspect of the program.

For this reviewing technique, ask participants to gather around the cards and internally process each of the five themes represented by the cards, and then be willing to share one of their insights with the group.

Partner Watch

OBJECTIVE
- To provide feedback

Group Size
Any

Materials
None

Time
20 to 30 minutes

Procedure

Here is a reviewing technique that is sure to provide a higher level of feedback than almost any other technique. Think of this as a very simple, one-person version of 360-degree feedback. It can be used with almost any size group, from 2 to 200, and requires no additional props.

Partner Watch is an observation activity for partners and can be used with almost any activity in this book, with the possible exception of those that include blindfolds (which would limit the ability of observers to view their partners).

Begin by inviting everyone in the group to find a partner who they believe would give them honest feedback. Next, ask one person in each group of two to take the role of "receiver" in the following activity, while the other person in each pair takes the role of "observer."

For the purpose of this reviewing technique, both partners are active participants in the activity but have specific tasks. The receiver is encouraged to participate in the task exactly as he or she typically would. The observer also participates, perhaps taking a bit more passive role than usual but intently watching the participation of his or her partner, specifically with the goal of being able to provide the partner with feedback related to the partner's performance during the activity. It can be helpful for the observer to stand a distance away from their subject, to allow adequate observation and to limit interference.

Next, engage the group in the activity of choice. After the activity is complete, invite everyone to find their partners, and instruct the receivers to ask their partners for feedback about their performance. Receivers can ask specific questions such as "Was my voice too forceful when I offered my idea?" Observers should be prepared to share the most relevant details they recall, such as "I noticed that you helped the group more in the idea-generation stage than during the actual completion of the task."

When the first activity and partner feedback are complete, invite the members of each group to switch roles and introduce the next activity.

It is generally best to have partners switch roles during two different activities, rather than attempting to have both partners deliver feedback for their partner during the same activity. This procedure will reduce what is known as the Hawthorne effect or the participant-observer effect, where participants sometime alter their behavior simply because they are being observed. Two people, each participating in the same activity while observing the other, are likely to be so focused on the observation of the other that their own participation varies, sometimes dramatically, from their typical behavior in a group. In one extreme case, each person would say, "I observed you watching me." At the other end of the spectrum, each person would say, "I was so involved with the activity I forgot to observe you." The optimal case is one where the observer has sufficient time to watch their partner while participating in the activity, and their partner is sufficiently involved with the activity to not notice that their partner is watching him or her.

Highs and Lows

OBJECTIVE

- To provide reviewing frameworks

Group Size

Up to 20

Materials

Masking tape

Time

10 minutes

Procedure

The value of a debriefing or reviewing framework is to provide participants with a general theme for which to reflect on their experiences. This creative approach, which is often new to many participants, moves beyond the general evaluation process of a program or training event and encourages deeper consideration of the teachable moments experienced.

For such techniques to have value, the facilitator needs to frame the reviewing and reflection process with one of the following themes. Recording the responses to each of these themes on a flip-chart page can provide your participants with a written record of their experiences and perhaps the beginning of a plan for the future. You can also designate a location for each theme and invite participants to reflect on their experiences and then join the group that best identifies their findings.

Highs and Lows

This simplest of frameworks encourages participants to reflect on their personal high and low points for the program and then share these thoughts with others. As a nonverbal alternative to this method, tape a single line on the floor with "High" at one end and "Low" at the other. Next, invite participants to stand along the line at a position that adequately reflects their experience for the day.

Plus/Delta

This alternative to the basic Highs and Lows process previously described places a more positive framework on the experience. In this case, participants are asked to reflect on the positive aspects of the event and on things they would change or alter.

PMI

This trio of themes—plus, minus, and interesting—is attributed to Edward De Bono and also extends the basic High and Low framework by including a place where interesting, surprising, and unusual themes can reside. When this technique is employed with most groups, a significantly higher number of responses are present in the "interesting" category than in the other two combined.

BDA

The final technique in this collection of reviewing activities is framed by things that happened before, during, or after the program. Participants might reflect, for example, that prior to the start of the program they were excited or a bit nervous. While some participants will choose a single time frame for their comments in this activity, some may choose to address all three. The simplicity of this technique allows greater participation by all members of the group.

Tweeting

Group Size

Any

Materials

Tweet Your Experience worksheet, pen

Time

15 minutes

Procedure

With the proliferation of cell phones, social media, email, texting, and other continually advancing forms of communication, it is no surprise that the total number of messages sent increases every day. Statistics indicate that the total number of messages sent each day is actually greater than the total number of people on the planet! Futurists have remarked that as the number of messages increases, the total amount of information conveyed in those messages will proportionally diminish.

This theory was well illustrated by the introduction of Twitter (www .twitter.com). In messages limited to 140 total characters, millions of people have found a method for communicating. A few years ago, the task of creating a concise mission or vision statement for your corporation encouraged concise language. The more concise and clearer the wording, the better. Decades ago, newspapers featured printed want ads that were frequently charged per word or per line. Shorter want ads were significantly cheaper than longer ones. And a century ago, telegraph operators charged per word for messages they sent using their then-state-of-the-art communication technique.

The important factor in each of these methods is to be able to concisely convey the information you desire with a limited number of words. We'll use that same technique in this reviewing process.

On the following page, you'll find a blank message page with exactly 140 available spaces. You will no doubt need several of these pages to allow for editing, corrections, and creative additions. Use this page with your group to create a single message that will encompass the sum total of your experience today. Feel free to use abbreviations, slang, and/or other now-common text-messaging words and phrases. Bonus points if your team can complete the task in less than 100 characters.

Tweet Your Experience

In 140 characters or less, create a message that will summarize your experience today.

7

The Right Stuff: Finding the References, Props, Tools, and Equipment You Need

One ought, every day at least, to hear a little song, read a good poem, see a fine picture, and, if it were possible, to speak a few reasonable words.

—Johann Wolfgang von Goethe

This chapter focuses on additional information and tools that can help you improve your skills. You can find many of the printed resources and books in your local public library system or bookstores. Internet resources are available online, and all the activity props, equipment, and tools listed in this book can be easily assembled from local resources or suggested vendors, or handmade yourself.

References

Reading That Encourages and Inspires

During the preparation of this book for publication, we reviewed hundreds of books, articles, and electronic documents in search of the very best activities and practices in training, teaching, and facilitating groups. Here you will find a concise listing of the best of the best: a handful of publications and resources that contain valuable information, inspiration, and helpful suggestions that are sure to make you better in this craft. You'll also find other publications by us, so that you can continue to learn from them. These publications contain even more of the activities and techniques used by us in our roles as trainers, teachers, facilitators, and consultants.

Big Book of Brainstorming Games, Mary Scannell and Mike Mulvihill, New York: McGraw-Hill, 2012.
>   Unleash your team's creative power with games that engage all personality types.

Big Book of Conflict Resolution Games, Mary Scannell, New York: McGraw-Hill, 2010.
>   Learn to turn conflicts into opportunities for collaboration, all while building trust and respect.

Big Book of Team-Motivating Games, Mary Scannell and Ed Scannell, New York: McGraw-Hill, 2009.
>   Games to increase engagement, improve communication, and get your team fired up!

Big Book of Virtual Team-Building Games, Mary Scannell, Michael Abrams, and Mike Mulvihill, New York: McGraw-Hill, 2012.
>   Activities to connect your team members, even when they are separated by space and time.

"Developmental Sequence in Small Groups," Bruce Tuckman, *Psychological Bulletin* 63, no. 6 (1965): 384–399.
  The classic original article from the researcher who coined the terms *forming, storming, norming,* and *performing.*
"Developmental Sequence in Small Groups," *Group Facilitation: A Research and Applications Journal* 3, Bruce W. Tuckman, Spring (2001): 66–81.
  A look back, 35 years after the original groundbreaking article. Required reading for all group facilitators. In this article Tuckman himself mentions that most of the initial research and data collected on this subject was provided from therapy groups rather than natural work teams. In support of this research, however, many natural work groups could genuinely benefit from therapeutic techniques!
Educating for Character: How Our Schools Can Teach Respect and Responsibility, Thomas Lickona, New York: Bantam Books, 1991.
  Teaching character and more.
Effective Training Strategies, James R. Davis and Adelaide B. Davis, San Francisco: Berrett-Koehler Publishers, 1998.
  A comprehensive guide to maximizing learning in organizations.
The Empty Bag: Non-Stop, No-Prop Adventure-Based Activities for Community Building, Dick Hammond and Chris Cavert, FUNdoing Publications, 2003.
  Amazing things to do with no props at all!
Essential Staff Training Activities, Jim Cain, Clare-Marie Hannon, and David Knobbe, Dubuque, IA: Kendall Hunt Publishing, 2009.
  One of the best active staff training books on the planet.
Experiential Learning: Experience as the Source of Learning and Development, David Kolb, Upper Saddle River, NJ: FT Press, 1983.
  The classic volume on experiential learning.
Flow: The Psychology of Optimal Experience, Mihaly Csikszentmihalyi, New York: HarperCollins, 1990.
  A classic view of the ideal place between boredom and anxiety.
The Leadership Moment, Michael Useem, New York: Three Rivers Press, 1998.
  Nine true stories of triumph and disaster and their lessons for us all.
Made to Stick: Why Some Ideas Survive and Others Die, Chip Heath and Dan Heath, New York: Random House, 2007.

These authors introduce the SUCCESs model for creating an interesting learning environment.

Multiple Intelligences in the Classroom, 3rd edition, Thomas Armstrong, Alexandria, VA: ASCD, 2009.

This is an excellent template for designing your own curriculum with multiple possibilities for reviewing and learning in different ways.

The Not So Big Life, Sarah Susanka, New York: Random House, 2007.

Making room for what really matters.

Outliers: The Story of Success, Malcolm Gladwell, New York: Little, Brown & Company, 2008.

With 10,000 hours of practice, you too can become an expert!

Play, Stuart Brown, and Christopher Vaughan, New York: Avery Publishers, 2009.

How play shapes the brain, opens the imagination, and invigorates the soul.

"Practices That Support Teacher Development," Ann Lieberman, *Phi Delta Kappan* 76, no. 8 (1995): 591–596.

A selection of learning opportunities to engage teachers in experiencing, creating and solving real problems, using their own experiences and working with others.

Research-Based Strategies to Ignite Student Learning, Judy Willis, Alexandria, VA: ASCD, 2006.

Insights from a neurologist and classroom teacher.

The Revised & Expanded Book of Raccoon Circles, Jim Cain and Tom Smith, Dubuque, IA: Kendall Hunt Publishing, 2007.

More than 200 simple activities that explore community building, social capital, and creative problem solving, using just a piece of tubular webbing.

Shouting Won't Grow Dendrites: 20 Techniques for Managing a Brain-Compatible Classroom, Marcia L. Tate. Thousand Oaks, CA: Corwin Press, 2006.

Outstanding book on brain-based learning.

"Sit and Get" Won't Grow Dendrites: 20 Professional Learning Strategies That Engage the Adult Brain, Marcia L. Tate, Thousand Oaks, CA: Corwin Press, 2004.

Brain research focused on the adult learner.

Smart Moves: Why Learning Is Not All in Your Head, Carla Hannaford, Arlington, VA: Great Ocean Publishers, 1995.
A great presentation of why active learning works.

Social Intelligence, Daniel Goleman, New York: Bantam Dell, 2006.
The new science of human relationships.

The Speed of Trust, Stephen M. R. Covey, New York: Free Press, 2006.
Trust is the one thing that changes everything!

"Stages of Small-Group Development Revisited," *Group and Organizational Studies* 2, no. 4 (1977): 419–427, Bruce Tuckman and Mary Ann Jenson. This article added the fifth stage of group development known as adjourning.

A Teachable Moment: A Facilitator's Guide to Activities for Processing, Debriefing, Reviewing and Reflection, Jim Cain, Michelle Cummings, and Jennifer Stanchfield.. Dubuque, IA: Kendall Hunt Publishing, 2005. Adventure-based and active learning activities open the door for meaningful conversations about subjects that matter. Learn how to go beyond just the activities with these tools.

Teambuilding Puzzles, Mike Anderson, Jim Cain, Chris Cavert, and Tom Heck, Dubuque, IA: Kendall Hunt Publishing, 2005.
Engaging activities that you can use to reinforce essential life skills, corporate skills, and core values.

Teamwork & Teamplay, Jim Cain and Barry Jolliff, Dubuque, IA: Kendall Hunt Publishing, 1998.
A guide to challenge and adventure activities that build cooperation, teamwork, creativity, trust, communication, and creative problem-solving skills. Award-winning team-building knowledge and expertise.

Telling Ain't Training, Harold D. Stolovitch and Erica J. Keeps, Alexandria, VA: ASTD Press, 2002.
In addition to fascinating information about training, this book also has an extensive bibliography of additional references.

Theories of Small Group Development, 4th edition, Raye Kass, Concordia University, 2010.
For trainers and consultants interested in maximizing team effectiveness.

Training on Trial, James D. Kirkpatrick, and Wendy Kayser Kirkpatrick, New York: AMACOM, 2010.

A wake-up call for how workplace learning must reinvent itself to remain relevant.

Values Clarification: A Practical, Action-Directed Workbook, Sidney B. Simon, Leland W. Howe, and Howard Kirschenbaum. New York: Warner Books, 1995.

The classic guide to discovering your truest feelings, beliefs, and goals.

Vital Friends, Tom Rath, New York: Gallup Press, 2006.

Ammunition for proving the value of friendship in the corporate world.

Worksheets Don't Grow Dendrites, Marcia L Tate, Thousand Oaks, CA: Corwin Press, 2003. Twenty instructional strategies that engage the brain.

Websites

www.funderstanding.com	Whole-brain teaching techniques.
www.reviewing.co.uk	Roger Greenaway's excellent website filled with a wide variety of techniques for reviewing, debriefing, and reflection.
www.training-wheels.com	Michelle Cumming's website, where you can order most of the equipment used in this book.
www.teamworkandteamplay.com	Author Jim Cain's team-building website. In addition to some great team-building ideas, this site also has a collection of free, downloadable instructions for activities and playful equipment that you can make yourself.

Activity Props, Tools, and Equipment

The more talented somebody is, the less they need the props.
—*Hugh McLeod,* How to Be Creative

We have attempted to minimize the total number of training props required to facilitate each of the activities in this book. Below you will find a list of this equipment along with recommendations on how to create this equipment yourself, or how to purchase it directly from suppliers around the world.

Equipment Description	Activities
Raccoon Circle—15-foot (4.6 m) segments of tubular that sell climbing gear, and also available at horse tack shops.	Over Here! Wrapped Around My Finger Where Ya From, Where Ya Been? Twice Around the Block My Lifeline All My Life's a Circle The Goal Line, Inside/Out A Knot Between Us The Missing Link
Index cards	Character Cards Alphabet Soup Back Writing Active Quotations Word Circles 13 Clues Changing Places
Handouts (Originals are available in this book)	The Big Question The Big Answer

Equipment Description	Activities
Music	The Leadership Dance
Tarps, tablecloths, or shower curtains	Sunny Side Up Magic Carpet
Playing cards	Playing Card Debrief 16-Card Puzzle
Stopwatch	Four-Minute Team
100-foot-long (30 m) rope	"Un-Blind" Square Step into the Circle The Fishbowl
Activities that require no equipment include:	The Story of Your Name Story Stretch Magic Pot, Over Here! Walk and Talk The Trust Drive Where Do You Stand? A Knot Between Us Bobsled Team Partner Watch Pairing and Sharing "I'm In"

Special or Unique Equipment

PVC Teamplay Tubes are a unique collection of 50 PVC tubes and connectors and are available at www.training-wheels.com.

The PVC Construction Project

A bull ring is a 1.5-inch-diameter (3.8 cm) metal ring with colorful strings. This device can be used to transport a tennis or golf ball. The candelabra is constructed using Teamplay Tubes and is available at www.training-wheels.com.

Bull Ring Candelabra

Character Cards are produced by Creative Concepts and are available at www.training-wheels.com.

Character Cards

Zoom is a book by Istvan Banyai. There is also a second book in this series entitled *Re-Zoom*.

Zoom

Petecas are associated with Brazil but are also found in many countries around the world. They are available for purchase at www.training-wheels.com or you can download "The Featherball" document at www.teamworkandteamplay.com to make your own peteca.

Peteca

You can use the illustration shown in the Tangram template in this book to create your own tangrams, or purchase them at game, craft, or educational supply stores.

Tangrams

Credits

Story Stretch, Pairing and Sharing, and the no-prop version of Lighthouse were first published in Jim Cain's no-prop book *Find Something to Do*.

Over Here! is based on the activity See Ya! by Chris Cavert and is used here with his permission. You will find this activity in his book *The Empty Bag*. For more information about this activity and other valuable training ideas, visit www.fundoing.com.

The Story of Your Name, Walk and Talk, The Big Question, The Big Answer, a variation of the Bobsled Team known as The Change Train, Character Cards, Bull Ring Candelabra, Sunny Side Up, The Leadership Dance, Alphabet Soup, Peteca, PVC Construction Project, The Trust Drive (activity description and script), and Active Quotations were first published in the book *Essential Staff Training Activities* by Jim Cain, Clare-Marie Hannon, and Dave Knobbe.

Back Writing, as it appears here, is based upon the activity Back Art by Tom Jackson and is used here with his permission. You'll find this activity in his book *Activities That Teach*. For more information about these activities and other valuable training ideas, visit www.activelearning.org or contact Tom at tjackson@netutah.com or by calling (435) 586-7058.

The Magic Carpet activity presented here first appeared in the book Teamwork & Teamplay by Jim Cain and Barry Jolliff. The goal-setting version first appeared in the book *Essential Staff Training Activities* by Jim Cain, Clare-Marie Hannon, and Dave Knobbe.

Word Circles are based upon the early work of Chip Schlegel and further improved by Chris Cavert. The best resource currently available on Word Circles is the Word Circles Puzzle Kit—The Challenge That Never Ends by Chris Cavert. This PDF and paper format collection of Word Circle puzzles is available from Training Wheels, Inc. at www.training-wheels.com.

Community Juggling and Handcuffs first appeared in the book *Teamwork & Teamplay* by Jim Cain and Barry Jolliff.

Partner Watch, and The Magic Pot as it appears here, were first presented in the book *A Teachable Moment* by Jim Cain, Michelle Cummings, and Jennifer Stanchfield.

Four-Minute Team, "Un-Blind" Square, and The Fishbowl were first published in *The Ropework & Ropeplay Collection of Team Activities* by Jim Cain.

Raccoon Circle Games, A Knot Between Us, The Missing Link, Inside/Out, 13 Clues, and Step into the Circle were first published in *The Revised and Expanded Book of Raccoon Circles* by Jim Cain and Tom Smith.

The Raccoon Circle activities Twice Around the Block and My Lifeline were first published in the Internet version of Raccoon Circle activities, available for free online at www.teamworkandteamplay.com.

Playing Card Debrief and 16-Card Puzzle presented here were first published as an activity with the *Teamwork & Teamplay Character Cards* by Jim Cain. Card activities such as The Big Question, Character Cards, Back Writing, Alphabet Soup, Snowflakes, Zoom, Active Quotations, Word Circles, Tweeting, and fifty more appear in the book *It's All in the Cards* by Jim Cain.

"I'm In" Games, Blind Shapes, Arrowheads, A Quick Study, Modern Hieroglyphics, and Changing Places were first published in the book *Teambuilding Puzzles* by Mike Anderson, Jim Cain, Chris Cavert, and Tom Heck.

About the Authors

Mary Scannell

 A training consultant with 20 years of experience in developing, designing, and delivering training programs, Mary specializes in delivering high-value training that is cost effective and time efficient. She has worked with all levels of staff, from senior executives to entry-level employees. Known for her high-energy style, she attributes her ability to keep trainees engaged throughout the session to her use of the training activities found in this book.

Mary's expertise in games and group activities extends through the full gamut of the topic—from small classroom exercises to large-scale outdoor adventure events. She is an active member of her community, and for over a decade has worked with a local nonprofit to help Arizona youth become more connected to their schools, their homes, and their communities (educationalendeavors.com), through the use of experiential activities and ropes-course initiatives.

Mary is a member of the American Society for Training and Development. She received a B.S. from the W. P. Carey School of Business at Arizona State University.

Find out more about Mary Scannell at bizteamtools.com; or to contact Mary, call 602-663-7788 or email mary@maryscannell.com.

Jim Cain

 **Jim Cain, Ph.D.,** is the author of the team- and community-building texts *Teamwork & Teamplay, The Revised and Expanded Book of Raccoon Circles, Teambuilding Puzzles, A Teachable Moment, Essential Staff Training Activities, Find Something to Do, It's All in the Cards,* and this book, *The Big Book of Low-Cost Training Games.* He is a former executive director of the Association for Challenge Course Technology (ACCT); a senior consultant to the Cornell University Corporate Teambuilding Program; and the founder, director, and creative force behind his training company, Teamwork & Teamplay. Dr. Cain frequently serves as a staff development specialist on building unity, community, connection, leadership, corporate culture, engagement and teamwork. He has shared his knowledge with individuals and organizations in 47 states and 23 countries (so far).

Jim Cain
Teamwork & Teamplay
468 Salmon Creek Road
Brockport, NY 14420 USA
Phone (585) 637-0328
jimcain@teamworkandteamplay.com
www.teamworkandteamplay.com